OCCUPATIONAL HAZARDS

Stephen Brown
OCCUPATIONAL HAZARDS

Based on the memoir by
Rory Stewart

OBERON BOOKS
LONDON

WWW.OBERONBOOKS.COM

First published in 2017 by Oberon Books Ltd
521 Caledonian Road, London N7 9RH
Tel: +44 (0) 20 7607 3637 / Fax: +44 (0) 20 7607 3629
e-mail: info@oberonbooks.com
www.oberonbooks.com

Occupational Hazards: My Time Governing in Iraq © Rory Stewart, 2006

Adaptation © Stephen Brown, 2017

Stephen Brown is hereby identified as author of this play in accordance with section 77 of the Copyright, Designs and Patents Act 1988. The author has asserted his moral rights.

All rights whatsoever in this play are strictly reserved and application for performance etc. should be made before commencement of rehearsal to United Agents, 12-26 Lexington Street, London, W1F 0LE. No performance may be given unless a licence has been obtained, and no alterations may be made in the title or the text of the play without the author's prior written consent.

You may not copy, store, distribute, transmit, reproduce or otherwise make available this publication (or any part of it) in any form, or binding or by any means (print, electronic, digital, optical, mechanical, photocopying, recording or otherwise), without the prior written permission of the publisher. Any person who does any unauthorized act in relation to this publication may be liable to criminal prosecution and civil claims for damages.

A catalogue record for this book is available from the British Library.

PB ISBN: 9781786821720
E ISBN: 9781786821737

Printed and bound by 4edge Limited, UK.

Visit www.oberonbooks.com to read more about all our books and to buy them. You will also find features, author interviews and news of any author events, and you can sign up for e-newsletters so that you're always first to hear about our new releases.

Occupational Hazards was first performed on 28 April 2017 at Hampstead Theatre, London, with the following cast:

AHMED	Nezar Alderazi
MUSAB	Waj Ali
KARIM	Silas Carson
RIFAT	Vangelis Christodoulou
JT	Amy Cudden
ABU RASHID/KHALED	Vincent Ebrahim
RANA	Aiysha Hart
RORY STEWART	Henry Lloyd-Hughes
THE COLONEL/BREMER	John Mackay
SEYYED HASSAN	Johndeep More

Director	Simon Godwin
Designer	Paul Wills
Lighting	Oliver Fenwick
Sound	Alex Caplen
Music	Khyam Allami
Projection	Zakk Hein
Movement	John Ross
Casting	Suzanne Crowley and Gilly Poole
Assistant Director	Emily Burns

Characters

RORY STEWART
Former diplomat, to be appointed Governorate Co-ordinator for the province of al-Amarah. Scotsman, 30 years old.

THE COLONEL
Commanding officer of the British Army Battle Group in Maysan province, Scotsman, 45 years old.

AHMED
An Iraqi translator / assistant working for the British in al-Amarah. Early 20s.

KARIM MAHOOD
Aka 'The Prince of the Marshes', a famed resistance fighter against Saddam. A Marsh Arab and tribal sheikh. 40.

ABU RASHID
Cousin of Karim, who fought with him in the resistance. Made Police Chief of Maysan by the Colonel. 45.

RANA BASHIR
Iraqi woman running a project in al-Amarah to teach women to sew. Daughter of Khaled. 30 years old.

KHALED BASHIR
Professor of history at al-Amarah University. Father of Rana. 50s.

SEYYED HASSAN
A preacher and leader of the Sadrist Movement in al-Amarah. 30.

MUSAB
A poor former factory worker, living in Mu'allimin, a slum area of al-Amarah. Brother of Rifat. 30.

RIFAT
A poor former factory foreman, also living in Mu'allimin. Brother of Musab. 30.

AMBASSADOR PAUL BREMER
State Department veteran, appointed to run the Coalition Provisional Authority, American, 62, looks 50.

MAJOR ED MELOTTE
Officer in the Irish Guards, running British Army's reconstruction effort in Maysan before Rory's arrival. 37.

JT
British Soldier, 25, Captain, female, TA, part of the civil affairs team with the battle group stationed in al-Amarah.

Also: British soldiers, Sadrist militia, Council members.

Staging should be flexible and/or sparse, allowing for rapid scene changes. Descriptions of locations are for information and to inspire design ideas. Location need not be literally represented.

The play is set in and around al-Amarah, a city of around 300,000 people in southern Iraq. Al-Amarah is a mostly modern city, built on a grid pattern, running along the banks of the river Tigris. Around it is farmland, desert, what remains of the marshlands of southern Iraq, oilfields and a refinery.

NOTES ON CHARACTERS

RORY STEWART is a small, quirky man. He is dressed in a dark birds-eye suit, with a blue, open-necked shirt, cuff links, brogue boots.

The COLONEL is in his mid-40s, ex-special forces, bullish, wiry, desert combat fatigues.

KARIM is tall, handsome, dramatic, imposing. He is dressed in a top-of-the-range Kuwaiti Bedouin robe with gold trim, and neat headdress. Very much the picture book 'tribal sheikh' – which is the intended effect. He wears a side arm. He gives off the feeling that something dangerous may happen at any moment.

ABU RASHID is an overweight, jovial man, bearded, battle-hardened but with something of Santa Claus about him, straining out of his policeman's uniform.

AHMED works as a translator for the British. He's a quick young Iraqi English Lit graduate in a leather jacket and jeans.

JT is a young female British Army reservist, who has learned how to live in a very male world.

RANA is a self-possessed Iraqi woman, dressed in public in a black abaya and hijab, but with flashes of Baghdad style, jewellery perhaps, when location allows.

MUSAB, a man with slicked back hair, a thick anorak, frayed cheap trousers, heavy plastic sandals. He is dressed in a counterfeit 'Reebook' tracksuit.

RIFAT is a poor former factory worker, living in the rough part of al-Amarah. Poor but better dressed than MUSAB.

SEYYED HASSAN is the senior Sadrist in al-Amarah. He is wearing a woollen cloak, a black turban, and has a large beard. He talks quietly and with a compelling inner certainty.

KHALED is an academic in his 50s. He has rather long, raffish hair and a goatee beard. He's wearing a corduroy jacket, spectacles.

BREMER is dressed in chinos, navy blazer, tan Timberland boots, white shirt and tie. Confident.

A NOTE ON THE TRUTH

Though this play is based on Rory Stewart's memoir and other research, it should not be taken as a historical record. Some characters and incidents have been adapted or invented for dramatic purposes.

This text went to press during rehearsals and so may differ from the script as performed.

Act One

THE CONFIDENCE OF YOUTH

RORY speaks to us.

RORY: Welcome, people of Hampstead!

> Thank you for coming today.
>
> My name is Rory Stewart.
>
> I'm the MP for Penrith and the Borders. I'm Minister of State at the Department for International Development.
>
> But this story is not about now.
>
> This is a story about my time governing in Iraq, after the invasion.
>
> It's the truth. Mostly.
>
> You could say it's about…

SPEAKER 1: The confidence of youth.

RORY: Think back to the time before the invasion of Iraq.

SPEAKER 2: When Germany reunified…

SPEAKER 3: When the Good Friday Agreement was signed…

SPEAKER 4: When the fragile democracy of Sierra Leone was restored…

RORY: For that moment, wouldn't you say the whole of the West had the confidence of youth?

> *INTO:*

PLANTING TREES

RORY talking to us.

Around him, on stage, all the other actors.

RORY: *(Out.)* It is April 2002. After twenty months walking in Asia, I return to my home in the Highlands of Scotland, a mile from the nearest town, on the edge of a wood. I begin to turn my experiences walking across Afghanistan into a book. I plant four hundred trees.

(Out.) It is March 2003. I watch the invasion of Iraq on TV. I'm not in the Foreign Office anymore. I resigned. But I send in my CV anyway.

RORY looks at the other actors. Nothing.

RORY: No one replies. In August, I fly to Jordan and take a taxi from Amman to Baghdad to ask for a job.

We are now in Baghdad, the Green Zone. A hive of activity.

RORY: *(Out.)* A friend from my time in the Balkans gets me into the Green Zone, where the Coalition has assembled a temporary government for Iraq – the Coalition Provisional Authority – in Saddam's complex of palaces in the centre of the city. There are proverbs in Arabic on the walls. One reads:

SPEAKER 1: Ask not what your country can do for you, but what you can do for your country.

RORY: *(Out.)* Signed:

SPEAKER 2: Saddam Hussein.

Ambassador PAUL 'JERRY' BREMER steps forward.

BREMER: Our mission is to turn Iraq from a symbol of tyranny into a beacon of freedom.

RORY: *(Out.)* On my second day I secure a meeting with Ambassador Paul Bremer –

BREMER: – My friends call me Jerry –

RORY: *(Out.)* – the state department veteran appointed to run the CPA –

BREMER: Our mission is to build a multi-ethnic, decentralised, prosperous state, based on human rights, a just constitution and the rule of law.

RORY: *(Out.)* On his desk is a plaque with the words:

BREMER: 'Success has a thousand fathers'.

RORY: *(Out.)* Omitted is the second half of the quotation: 'But failure is an orphan'.

BREMER: I read your CV!

RORY: You did?

BREMER: You were flying high. FCO fast track – Indonesia – UK rep in Montenegro. And then you went walking for two years?

RORY: I like walking.

BREMER: As explanations go, that seems necessary but not sufficient. Still –

RORY: *(Out.)* It so happens that the CPA has just realised they need to do something about the provinces.

BREMER: We'd like you to be one of our 'Governorate Co-ordinators'.

RORY: Governorate what, sorry?

BREMER: For Maysan province. Not a headline province of course –

RORY: I know Maysan.

BREMER: You do?

RORY: Where the Marsh Arabs are. I read about them as a boy.

BREMER: Right! We've got a great guy from the Marshes helping us down there. Maybe you heard of him, Karim Mahood, fought against Saddam in the resistance. A national hero. Working with us to build a modern, secular Iraq. Kind of man reminds you why we're doing all this.

RORY: When you say 'Governorate Co-ordinator', do you mean 'governor'?

BREMER: The governor has to be an Iraqi. But you'll have all the powers of a governor. All right, you got me. Effectively, governor. Don't tell anyone I said that! You want it?

RORY: *(Out.)* I am thirty years old.

Beat.

RORY: *(Out.)* Within days I'm in Basra at what used to be the civilian airport and now serves as Coalition headquarters in the south. There are flies everywhere. I'm issued with a helmet, body armour, and –

A soldier hands RORY these items –

(Out.) A skimpy green towel –

RORY holds it up to show how tiny it is –

SOLDIER: *(Cough.)*

RORY: *(Out.)* And I'm given advice on the challenges of life in Iraq –

SOLDIER: Now you will notice as you pass your days in the beautiful country of Iraq that it is fucking full of flies. You will put out blue bowls of poison paste. You will spray military grade insecticide delivered through highly technical fogging machines. These will make you sick. You will sweep away the little bastards' dead bodies. And half an hour later the fuckers will have returned. At this point you should remember my further advice: stop being a whingeing civilian prick!

The SOLDIER slaps her neck to kill a fly.

RORY: *(Out.)* I report to what used to be some kind of souvenir shop for a PowerPoint presentation on the province.

SOLDIER: Don't nick anything, sir.

During the scene RORY may purloin an abandoned souvenir.

MELOTTE: Welcome, Mufti of Maysan!

RORY: *(Out.)* Major Ed Melotte, Irish Guards. In charge of the British Army team running the province before my arrival.

MELOTTE: This is the most fun province in Iraq!

PowerPoint slide: A map of Maysan.

MELOTTE: Maysan is a province the size of Northern Ireland, roughly halfway between Basra and Baghdad. Al-Amarah, with a population of three hundred thousand, is the capital city of the province. The population is 99 per cent Shia Muslim.

New slide.

Water. Our water situation is ruined by the lack of electricity to power the pumps. Sewage. Sewage is at about 60 per cent.

RORY: *(Out.)* Does he mean it reaches 60 per cent of the population? That it works 60 per cent of the time? *(To MELOTTE.)* Excuse me –

New slide.

MELOTTE: Electricity. Our greatest challenge. We have a gang of looters using tractors to pull down electricity pylons. We've got a grid damaged by war –

RORY: And so it went on for two hours, until the Major brought up his final PowerPoint slide –

Powerpoint slide: A Marsh Arab in his canoe, silhouetted at sunset, fishing.

MELOTTE: Now. You've probably heard of our local Robin Hood?

RORY: Karim Mahood?

MELOTTE: Bingo. Bravest man I ever met.

RORY: *(Out.)* Do I want it?

From here, the sound of a fly buzzing and the purple light of an 'Insect-o-cutor' – RORY and/or the other actors may look at the 'fly' as it moves around the stage.

RORY: Back in London my friends, many of whom marched against the war, try to dissuade me.

FRIEND 1: Ultimately, your boss is going to be George Bush. Think about that.

FRIEND 2: All this shit about Saddam's connection to nine-eleven.

RORY: My father, understandably horrified by my nearly freezing to death on my walk across Afghanistan, was not keen either.

DADDY: Really, darling, your mother and I thought you were going to settle down. Get a proper job. Meet a nice local girl. Produce some grandchildren.

RORY: I've worked in Indonesia and Yugoslavia and briefly in Afghanistan. I know post-conflict reconstruction is difficult.

I think Jerry Bremer's language sounds…overambitious. And like any right-thinking person, I'm suspicious of PowerPoint.

From here the buzzing of the fly and the humming and purple of the insect killer gets louder and brighter.

RORY: But I've walked with Iraqi Kurds who had fled from Saddam. I know what happened in Rwanda, where we did not intervene, and Kosovo and Sierra Leone, where we did.

DADDY: Remember, darling. Stop making decisions and you're dead.

SOLDIER holds out a rifle to RORY.

SOLDIER: For the drive up. Bullets come out of that end, sir.

By now the sound is very loud.

RORY: They're asking me to be Governorate Co-ordinator of Maysan Province, with executive, legislative and judicial authority over a population of nine hundred thousand people. Do I want it?

At home in Scotland I have planted four hundred trees: gean, Scots pine, box, rowan, oak.

By now RORY is grinning like an idiot.

(Almost shouting.) What do you think I'm going to do? Sit there and watch them grow?

The fly hits the Insect-o-cutor –

INTO:

THE PYLON

A ferocious crack as electricity from an overhead pylon electrocutes a man.

A hot morning in the desert outside al-Amarah. By the side of the road, at the base of an electricity pylon. A dead body, covered with a sheet, lies on the ground.

Onstage are: the COLONEL, KARIM MAHOOD, ABU RASHID, AHMED, RORY STEWART, and two British private soldiers, one with comms, standing guard.

KARIM MAHOOD and ABU RASHID have just arrived and are looking at the corpse. The COLONEL is next to KARIM. Their relationship is warm.

AHMED has positioned himself to interpret but his translations are assumed until they break down.

COLONEL: So?

KARIM: What kind of tribe leaves one of their men behind?

COLONEL: Poor bastard must have been lit up like a Christmas tree.

KARIM: Christmas tree?

COLONEL: Like a neon sign.

KARIM: So? I would have bitten through the wires with my teeth rather than abandon my friend.

COLONEL: That's why you're our kind of man, Karim.

RORY: *(Out.)* Day One. By the side of a desert road. Stretching to the horizon, a line of pylons pulled down by looters.

KARIM stoops down and pulls back the cloth to look at the charred head of the looter. The audience does not see it.

ABU RASHID: *(Horror, nausea.)* <<God is merciful!>>

AHMED: *(Staggering back.)* <<Fuck!>>

RORY does not recoil, steps forward to look more closely at the horrible sight.

COLONEL: Unbelievable! Number of bloody pylons they've pulled down you'd think they'd know how to do it by now.

KARIM: <<Our Iraqi electricity is learning how to defend itself.>>

AHMED: *(Recovering himself.)* Sorry Mr Rory! I've been sick a little. In my mouth.

RORY: That's quite alright.

KARIM lets the sheet drop, stands.

KARIM: Colonel. We can find these looters.

COLONEL: You can?

KARIM: I've heard stories. About a gang of men from prison. Criminal scum.

RORY: Were they released by Saddam? In the amnesty last year?

KARIM looks at RORY.

COLONEL: Ah. Karim, Abu Rashid. I want you to meet Rory Stewart. The new Governorate Co-ordinator I mentioned to you. Just got here this morning, wanted to come straight out, see how we do things.

RORY: Peace be upon you.

KARIM: *(Rudely not reciprocating RORY's greeting.)* You speak Arabic.

RORY: I do.

KARIM: And you're working on reconstruction?

RORY: Reconstruction and politics.

KARIM: Politics can wait! Al-Amarah needs money.

RORY: I know there've been some problems –

ABU RASHID: We have twelve police cars! And only nine of them have wheels!

KARIM: My men in the police haven't even been paid yet!

RORY: *(To COLONEL.)* The police haven't been paid? For how long?

COLONEL: Not since the invasion. We incorporated Karim's men into the police but Baghdad hasn't done the bloody paperwork yet.

ABU RASHID: Six months without pay!

KARIM: My men liberated this province from the Baathist vipers. They work to protect this city from Seyyed Hassan's terrorists and receive contempt in return.

RORY: I have excellent contacts in Baghdad.

ABU RASHID: We're very pleased you're here. I'm friends with everyone. Even Baghdad!

ABU RASHID extends his hand to RORY and RORY shakes it.

KARIM: I was expecting an American. The Americans have the money.

ABU RASHID: Abu Rashid. Chief of Police.

KARIM turns away from RORY to the COLONEL.

KARIM: My cousin in al Musharrah says this gang have been seen in the countryside around there. Colonel. If we launch raids immediately we can find them.

The COLONEL signals to the soldiers to gather round.

KARIM, ABU RASHID, AHMED and the COLONEL walk off into a huddle, their backs to RORY, a conversation we do not hear.

COLONEL: *(From his huddle with KARIM, ABU RASHID, AHMED, to one of the British soldiers.)* JT! Fetch the transport!

RORY: *(Out.)* Bad idea! In a war zone, when so much is uncertain, power is theatre.

RORY turns to KARIM.

Karim, son of Mahood, son of Hattab, Sheikh of the Albu Muhammad, the great Marsh Arab tribe of the South. Your name is known across Iraq for your brave fight against Saddam.

RORY has extended his hand.

RORY: I am the Coalition's senior representative in Maysan province. I answer directly to Ambassador Paul Bremer. The delay in paying your men is an insult, which I will put right. I will get the money.

Beat.

KARIM: When?

RORY: When? *(Out.)* Should've thought of that. It's the obvious next question. *(Then quickly, to KARIM.)* One week.

COLONEL: Rory, you've cleared – ?

RORY: In one week, I will have the pay for your men.

Beat: RORY's hand is still extended.

KARIM walks forward and grasps RORY's hand.

KARIM: Welcome to Maysan, the most beautiful province in Iraq.

RORY: I've always wanted to come here.

KARIM: You have?

RORY: I read about the marshes as a boy.

KARIM: You read Thesiger?

RORY: I loved that book.

KARIM: My grandfather hunted pigs with Thesiger!

RORY: Your grandfather knew Thesiger? Thesiger is one of my heroes.

KARIM: Ah Mr Robbie!

RORY: Rory –

KARIM: Mr Rory! Strange name. Thesiger is the crazy British writer I told you about, Colonel! Lived with my ancestors in the marshes for years. This is why we have had always such a friendship with the British. Because they are mad and they like hunting.

ABU RASHID: Friendship is everything.

KARIM: Come with me and my friend the Colonel and you will see the love between we Iraqis and the British – children waving – women giving flowers to soldiers –

ABU RASHID: And baklava! –

KARIM: Flowers, baklava. What a moment! We in the south of Iraq, we suffered under Saddam. I myself spent six years in Abu Ghraib. And yet now my men have liberated this city and we are here, working together, British and Iraqi, the Colonel, Mr Rory, Karim Mahood, building a new world, a free Iraq!

Enter JT, holding a comms unit, looking distraught.

COLONEL: Ready to go, JT?

JT: Yes and no sir… You know the pylons we replaced last week, on route six, sir?

COLONEL: I thought they were up and running?

JT: They were beautiful sir. It's just… While you were talking just now – *(Gesturing at the corpse.)* These fucking bastards, sir – they've gone right back there. Pulled them down.

INTO:

PETITIONERS

RORY: *(Out.)* Day Two. Another quiet day in the office. *(Sounds of the protestors outside.)*

AHMED: Rory –

JT: Rory, there's about a hundred protestors. Been at the gate since breakfast.

RORY: It's about the blackout?

JT: That's what they're chanting.

RORY: How hostile are they?

JT: Thrown a couple of bricks.

RORY: Can we open the gate?

JT: We can always open it. Question is, can we get it closed again?

AHMED: There are people waiting to get into the waiting room.

RORY: It's not too late to go back to the Colonel.

AHMED: I only ask myself: will you regret this so-called 'open door' policy?

RORY: Can you serve them coffee? I need to sort out this protest.

AHMED: Ok, then you're going to need this! *(Hands RORY bullet proof vest.)*

RORY: *(Refusing vest.)* Wrong look.

RANA: Governorate Co-ordinator. I run a dress-making course – for the women of al-Amarah. The Americans bought us the sewing machines – but now the Ministry of Education has taken the machines, says we need to pay for a licence.

RORY: *(To RANA.)* A licence? Who in the Ministry has said that?

RANA: *(Handing RORY a receipt.)* He gave us this as a receipt.

JT: Sir, we've got to go.

RORY: *(To RANA.)* Leave this with me.

    INTO:

THE CUT

In the auditorium, the noise of an angry crowd, chanting.

RORY stands in front of the crowd at the gates of the compound.

JT stands next to him.

RORY: *(Shouting to make himself heard.)* Peace be upon you. *(Shouting continues. Beat. RORY gets louder.)* PEACE BE UPON YOU! *(The crowd gets quieter.)* My name is Rory Stewart. I speak for the Coalition. Who speaks for you?

Voices from the crowd.

VOICES: Don't trust him! American scum! He's not American, he's British! British scum! He's lying!

JT: Maybe leave them to cool down, sir?

RORY: Who will speak to me?

A lobbed shoe arcs towards RORY.

RORY catches the shoe.

The crowd quietens.

RORY: *(Out.)* I'm not sure how I did that.

RORY puts the shoe gently on the ground next to him.

RORY: Who are your leaders?

RIFAT: I am the leader! I'm bringing my brother.

RORY: Fine. Come in here.

RIFAT: Fine.

Two brothers, RIFAT and MUSAB, come forward out of the crowd. (This might be from the audience itself.) Both men may smoke. RIFAT is leading MUSAB forward.

JT slams the gate shut behind them. Quiet.

RORY: Please, come through to my office.

RIFAT: We don't need an office!

RORY: In my office it is cooler. We have coffee?

RIFAT: We didn't come here to drink coffee!

MUSAB: *(Quietly, to RIFAT.)* I like coffee.

RIFAT: We came here to have our demands met.

RORY: OK. Then I am looking forward to hearing your demands right here, out in the sun.

RIFAT: Good. I am getting my demands.

MUSAB gives a pained apologetic wave to RORY.

RIFAT brings out a notebook.

RIFAT: *(At speed.)* The occupying forces have proved that greed, cruelty and ambition are their guiding ideals; that insensitivity and stupidity are the only qualifications for your administrators; cowardice and pusillanimity for your soldiers –

RORY: I'm sorry to interrupt. But could you tell me your demands?

Beat. RIFAT turns to another page in his notebook.

RIFAT: Number One! We demand reconstruction. There has been no building in this province!

RORY: There has been building.

RORY pulls a document from his pocket, shows it to the men. RIFAT shows no interest in it.

RORY: Al-Uzeyr primary school, seventeen thousand dollars, al-Amarah girls school –

RIFAT: Number Two! Jobs!

RORY: I agree that's an area where we need to do more.

RIFAT: We demand jobs!

RORY: But we have set up a jobs scheme –

RIFAT: That is for Karim Mahood's tribe!

RORY: No, it's not.

MUSAB: It is for Karim Mahood's tribe.

RORY: Right –

RIFAT: And you shut down the brick factory!

RORY: Wasn't the brick factory unsafe?

RIFAT: It was hell on earth! But it was a job!

    Number Three! Electricity.

MUSAB: Be calm, Rifat!

RIFAT: Two days without electricity! You bury us in darkness! –

RORY: That's because the looters have been pulling down the pylons –

RIFAT We see you on television! Mission Impossible! Titanic! How can you not solve this problem?

RORY: The electricity is complicated –

RIFAT: You are the greatest nation!

RORY: I think that's more the Americans nowadays.

RIFAT: *(Gesturing at MUSAB.)* And now my brother is injured!

RORY: I'm sorry to hear that.

RIFAT: Because of you! Because of you!

MUSAB: Please.

RIFAT: Tell him!

MUSAB: I said not to –

RIFAT: Tell him! The British need to know the truth!

MUSAB: I was shaving my pubic hair this morning, as the Prophet, peace be upon him, requires. And I…with the razor blade…I cut the tip of my penis. Off.

RORY: Right. That must be sore.

RIFAT: Because of you! Because of you!

RORY: That seems unlikely.

RIFAT: Have you tried to shave your pubic hair by torchlight?

RORY: No.

RIFAT: Look at us! We are educated men! We graduated from school! And now we are wearing these.

RIFAT pulls at MUSAB's trousers, which have a poorly faked 'Reebook' logo running down the leg.

MUSAB: *(Wincing.)* No! Don't touch my trousers!

RIFAT: Reebook! Is that right? It's not right. I know it's not right.

RIFAT: The coalition is an evil force! The British are ignoring us! We will never co-operate with you!

RORY: Can I answer your complaints now?

RIFAT: I have not come to hear your answers!

RORY: But then how can we speak?

Beat.

RIFAT: You make us look like fools! We will gather ten thousand men in the streets!

RIFAT hurtles off then comes back.

RIFAT: You are a capitalist imperialist crusader!

RIFAT hurtles off.

RORY: Your brother is very angry.

MUSAB: He fights to control himself.

RORY: Yes, I see.

Beat.

Would you like some coffee?

MUSAB: He was a good brother to me. But since we lost our jobs.

RORY: I'm sorry –

MUSAB: Seyyed Hassan is trying to help us –

RORY: Seyyed Hassan? In Mu'allimin?

MUSAB: You must know Seyyed Hassan.

RORY: Did Seyyed Hassan organise this demonstration?

MUSAB: My brother gathered us.

RORY: But you pray at Seyyed Hassan's mosque?

MUSAB: I should go.

RORY: *(Out.)* At first, it's a torrent of information – like a shoe being thrown at your head – but certain names you hear again and again – Seyyed Hassan. Seyyed Hassan.

RORY: Does Seyyed Hassan preach violence against the coalition?

MUSAB: He gives us food.

RORY: The gang that is pulling down electricity pylons, one of them was killed two days ago. If you've heard anything –

MUSAB: I shouldn't speak to you.

RORY: Wait!

RORY takes a twenty dollar bill from his wallet.

RORY: Have you been to the hospital? For your injury? The CPA is forbidden to give money to individuals. This is my personal gift. To thank you for welcoming me to your country.

MUSAB: I haven't welcomed you.

MUSAB takes the twenty dollar note.

MUSAB: The doctors want money for everything.

RORY: How much more will you need?

MUSAB: Another twenty?

RORY hands over another twenty dollar note.

RORY: This gang is hurting your people.

MUSAB: Abu Ali, he prays at mosque. They say the man who was electrocuted was his son.

RORY: You know this Abu Ali?

MUSAB: You need to talk to Seyyed Hassan.

RORY: We don't talk to Seyyed Hassan.

MUSAB: Why not?

RORY: Surely you…? *(Out.)* We don't talk to Seyyed Hassan because four months ago in the town of Majar al Kabir, south of here, his supporters marched on the police station and slaughtered six British soldiers. Soldiers who were there to train the local police.

MUSAB: I have to go.

RORY: Tell your brother: I'm going to change things. I'm here to help.

MUSAB leaves.

RORY: *(Out.)* That would make sense, wouldn't it? This gang of looters hiding in Mu'allimin. The part of the city we know the least well.

Seyyed Hassan. Radical Shia cleric. Leader of the Sadrists. No one in our team has met him.

COLONEL enters.

COLONEL: Seyyed Hassan is a vampire in holy clothing.

RORY: *(Out.)* But we can't wait. People are losing faith in us.

COLONEL: We've repaired two hundred schools!

RORY: They don't see that. They see that the electricity isn't working.

COLONEL: In Majar, Rory, at the police station. Six of my men, they died on their knees.

RORY: His mosque is giving out food parcels, kerosene –

COLONEL: You think terrorists don't do charity? The fucking IRA gives money to widows.

RORY: But we had to talk to the IRA, in the end. Didn't we?

INTO:

THE TRUTH

A room at SEYYED HASSAN's mosque, simply, even poorly furnished, perhaps some pictures of the iconic figures of Sadrism.

SEYYED HASSAN faces RORY.

RORY: I am glad to meet you, Seyyed.

Beat.

RORY: I know that you care for the future of your people. I've met people you've helped.

Beat.

RORY: We believe that some of the men who have been pulling down electricity pylons may be living in Mu'allimin. I'm here to ask for your help in finding them.

HASSAN: Rory Stewart, tell me, not as a British man, not as the C-P-A, but as a brother, how am I to speak to you and be considered your friend? When will the British Army cease its punishment of my people?

RORY: Do you preach violence against the British soldiers?

HASSAN: I seek only to teach the truth of Islam. We must uphold morality; we must care for the poor and sick; we must submit our lives to God.

RORY: Are you in revolution against the Coalition?

HASSAN: You say I am in revolution against the Occupation.

RORY: *(Out.)* The two words – 'occupation' and 'coalition' – are a couple of letters apart in Arabic. But I didn't mishear.

HASSAN: I only ever speak the truth.

RORY: *(Impulsively, almost under his breath, in English.)* But what is truth?

HASSAN: What did you say?

RORY: I said: 'what is truth?'

HASSAN: The Gospel of Saint John.

RORY: You know it?

HASSAN: Do you think I have read only one book? Pontius Pilate is interrogating the Prophet Jesus.

RORY: He needs to know if Jesus is a threat to the Roman state.

HASSAN: The Prophet Jesus insists his only purpose is to be a witness to the truth. Pilate asks: 'But what is it, this truth?'

RORY: And then he doesn't wait for Jesus to answer.

HASSAN: I don't think you're Pontius Pilate.

RORY: No, of course. I –

Beat.

This gang, Seyyed, the man who was electrocuted. We think his father may be in your congregation.

HASSAN: This is a smear from Karim Mahood.

RORY: This is nothing to do with Karim.

HASSAN: I would not protect men who hurt my own people.

RORY: The father is called Abu Ali.

HASSAN: Abu Ali? What's his proper name?

RORY: I don't have that but –

HASSAN: My congregation numbers a thousand men.

RORY: A thousand? Here?

Beat.

HASSAN: This is how you come to us? After one hundred days of silence. One hundred days while the British occupiers ignore our cries –

RORY: You know why that is –

HASSAN: One hundred days while your friend Karim Mahood steals money from you –

RORY: You have evidence of that?

HASSAN: You want me to prove this to you? To show you what's happening in your own house?

RORY: You know why the Colonel has no contact with you.

HASSAN: Because he has no respect for Islam.

RORY: It's because of what happened in Majar.

HASSAN: The British army raided a house in Majar on that day, the house of a preacher.

RORY: That doesn't justify killing six British military police officers. Those men were training Iraqi police.

HASSAN: Those men are the soldiers of an occupying army.

RORY: An army without which your movement would still be banned, its followers arrested.

HASSAN: We could have rid ourselves of Saddam –

RORY: The Shia rose up against Saddam in 1991. And they were slaughtered.

HASSAN: After your friend Bush's father broke his promise to help us.

RORY: Well, which do you want? To complain about us being here now, or failing to arrive then? If your people had risen up alone against Saddam, he would have blown you to dust.

Beat.

HASSAN: I regret what happened in Majar.

RORY: I think you're right about the Colonel. He hates you. Not only because of Majar, he hates everything about you – your faith, your beard – it terrifies him. But I've met men like you. I've walked with men like you. Help me find this gang. Show the British Army that we can work together. Let's build trust between us, one brick at a time.

SEYYED HASSAN walks away, digs out a brochure, comes back.

HASSAN: You know, Governorate Co-ordinator, these electricity thieves are only part of your problem. Even if you can catch them, this province will not have enough electricity.

RORY: Thats why we're planning a new power station. But it'll take two, three years.

HASSAN: Not if you buy one of these.

SEYYED HASSAN hands RORY a brochure.

HASSAN: It's a very large gas turbine. A portable power station. Install this at the refinery, connect it to the gas output, and, God willing, you will have forty megawatts new capacity overnight.

Beat.

HASSAN: Don't be surprised. I studied engineering before I heard the call. If used for the people's good, a machine like this can also be a praise of God.

RORY: This is a good beginning.

HASSAN: Is it? You talk of building trust, Mr Rory, while you govern a province with a corrupt tribal sheikh.

RORY: We're working towards a democracy.

HASSAN: Then where is this democracy? Where is one grain of it?

INTO:

BAKLAVA

RORY's office.

RORY: *(Out.)* I'm meeting with Karim and Abu Rashid. Topic: democracy.

AHMED enters with a large plate of baklava.

That's the best in al-Amarah?

AHMED: A man eating this cannot speak a sour word.

RORY arranges his desk. Laptop, phone, books etc.

He arranges them neatly on the desktop.

Stops to admire it.

AHMED: What are you doing?!

RORY: Arranging my desk.

AHMED: Don't put things on your desk! In Iraq, the emptier the desk, the more powerful the man.

RORY sweeps items on desk quickly into a drawer.

AHMED: You cannot fail.

AHMED rushes out again.

AHMED rushes back in again.

AHMED: Er Rory they're already here –

RORY finishes clearing his desk in a frenzy – AHMED puts down the baklava –

KARIM rushes in as RORY is stuffing his phone into the desk – followed at an easier pace by ABU RASHID –

Rapid, overlapping speech –

RORY: Peace be –

KARIM: Have you seen the wall?

RORY: I'm sorry the – ?

KARIM: The new wall! At the girls' school!

ABU RASHID: *(Nodding and smiling.)* Hello Rory! How are you?

RORY: I'm well, God be praised. And you?

ABU RASHID: I'm well thank you.

RORY: We had to finish that quickly Karim.

KARIM: I could push it over with my hand!

RORY: (I'm glad.) It's been inspected.

KARIM: If a cat walks on this wall it will fall over!

ABU RASHID: A big cat.

KARIM: When you need a builder, ask me!

RORY: I understand the Colonel has tended to follow your advice.

KARIM: Of course he has! How can a British man know who is a builder and who is a thief?

RORY shoots a look at the audience.

RORY grabs the plate of baklava and holds it out to his two guests.

RORY: Baklava?

ABU RASHID leans forward and grabs one –

KARIM: Are you trying to kill us all? This is full of sugar!

ABU RASHID: It's baklava!

RORY: It's the best in al-Amarah.

KARIM: It will clog up your arteries. It will fill your arteries with sugar and then one day quite suddenly you will die.

ABU RASHID: *(Who is happily eating a piece.)* Go on Karim.

KARIM: I'm trying to prolong your life.

RORY: On that note, Karim, sort of, I wanted to talk to you about the future of al-Amarah.

KARIM: A glorious future.

RORY: Yes… As you know, Iraq is on the journey to full democracy.

KARIM: After years of tyranny.

RORY: So. I want to give the people of al-Amarah more say in the running of this province.

KARIM: There can't be elections. Saddam perverted the census.

RORY: And the Constitution is still being debated in Baghdad. But I want to set up a Council of respected men and women in al-Amarah, to work with us running this province.

KARIM: The people of Iraq have had enough of politicians.

RORY: Iraq needs new politicians.

KARIM: The Colonel and I – and you – we're rebuilding. We keep the peace. Tomorrow we will find this gang –

RORY: You fought for this democracy, Karim. You and Abu Rashid and your men liberated this city from the Baathists. You made it possible. Now we need to take the next step.

KARIM: A council? That you choose? And then Baghdad will choose the governor?

RORY: I thought the council could elect the governor.

Beat.

KARIM nods.

KARIM: I know everyone in the province.

ABU RASHID: We're all friends.

RORY: We need to include representatives of all the major groups. The tribal leaders –

KARIM: That's essential –

RORY: The town mayors –

KARIM: There are some good men in this category –

ABU RASHID: My cousin is mayor of Maimuna –

RORY: The unions and chamber of commerce –

KARIM: They will argue with each other but OK –

RORY: Professionals –

ABU RASHID: I can give you a list of doctors –

RORY: The Sadrists –

KARIM: The what?

RORY: The Sadrists office.

KARIM: The followers of Seyyed Hassan? Seyyed Hassan is an illiterate, violent –

RORY: He's certainly not illiterate –

ABU RASHID: His men killed your soldiers, Rory.

RORY: That was a bad incident –

KARIM: It was the work of savages.

ABU RASHID: This is a misunderstanding.

KARIM: If you speak to Seyyed Hassan you'll see straightaway he's a dangerous man.

RORY: I've already spoken to him.

KARIM: Does the Colonel know this?

RORY: Of course. *(Out.)* More or less.

KARIM: Seyyed Hassan is a terrorist.

RORY: His rhetoric is violent, yes. But [the man himself] –

KARIM: 'Rhetoric'? This is your new name for a rifle?

RORY: If he is our enemy then we must hold him doubly close.

KARIM: Hold your enemies close? What kind of perversity is that?

RORY: If we exclude the Sadrists, they will only attack the Council from the outside –

KARIM: Then we attack them. We take our 'rhetoric' and we shoot them with it.

RORY: If we exclude the Sadrists, they will be able to blame you for everything that goes wrong without ever having to confront the difficult business of government. And there's something else. The man who was electrocuted, we think his father is in Seyyed Hassan's congregation.

ABU RASHID: You're sure of that?

RORY: Absolutely. *(Out.)* I mean, pretty sure.

ABU RASHID: You hope it.

RORY: Seyyed Hassan said he'd be happy to meet with you, Abu Rashid, to agree a plan.

ABU RASHID: He asked to speak to me by name?

KARIM: This is a mistake. We will find these men without the Sadrists help.

ABU RASHID: Though so far we've completely failed.

KARIM gets up to go.

KARIM: We have a saying here in Iraq, Rory. A fox pisses in the sea; and then he says: 'Look! The whole sea is made of my piss.'

RORY: You're saying I'm a fox pissing in the sea?

ABU RASHID: It means arrogance.

RORY: I got that.

KARIM: My men are risking their lives every day to protect this province and they haven't even been paid! That is how little respect your colleagues in Baghdad have for us. And then you talk of politics! I'm going to find the Colonel.

RORY lets KARIM walk away.

RORY: Of course – I'm sorry. I forgot.

RORY pulls a fat white envelope of cash out of his pocket and hands it to KARIM.

RORY: This is fifty thousand dollars. Please, pay your men.

Beat.

ABU RASHID: God is great!

RORY: The Coalition Provisional Authority apologises for the delay.

I made you a promise, Karim.

Beat.

ABU RASHID: Mr Rory. I, Abu Rashid of the Albu Muhammad, Police Chief of Maysan Province, this is my gift to you, to welcome you to Iraq, I will speak to Seyyed Hassan.

RORY: He suggested you could visit his mosque.

KARIM: The chief of police shouldn't be talking to known criminals!

ABU RASHID: The chief of police's business is with criminals. Besides, I'm friends with everyone. That's how I am.

KARIM: We're not actually friends with everyone.

ABU RASHID: Rory doesn't really like the Sadrists, Karim. He just wants to stop this gang.

RORY: That's not quite right –

ABU RASHID: You see! The British are the most cunning of all nations.

Beat.

ABU RASHID: When we were in the marshes, Rory, fighting Saddam, it was hard, but it was easy too. Our enemy was so clear. We killed him. He killed us. Being police is complicated! *(To KARIM.)* Come, dear Karim. Sit with our new friend.

KARIM sits back down, holds ABU RASHID's hand.

KARIM: This man broke me out of prison, Rory. When I was about to be executed.

ABU RASHID: I only drove the truck. And shot the guards. We will take you out into the marshes, those that Saddam did not destroy. Hunt wild pig – like our friend Thesiger –

KARIM: You know how to hunt?

RORY: I've hunted deer once or twice –

KARIM: The Colonel said the same thing!

ABU RASHID: A pig is different from a deer.

KARIM: If you don't kill him cleanly, he will rip your guts out with his tusks.

INTO:

CALM

RORY's office.

The end of a working day. Laptop and desk.

AHMED walks in carrying a blue bowl of insecticide paste.

RORY: What's that?

AHMED: For the flies!

RORY: *(Out.)* My mother keeps sending me links to articles about Iraq. The only thing they agree on is that we don't have a clue.

AHMED: What are you doing?

RORY: Emailing Baghdad. Telling them about the Council.

AHMED: You're saying about the Sadrists?

RORY: Not in detail. I'm saying we're adopting 'an inclusive approach'.

Beat.

RORY: I don't think anyone reads these emails anyway so –

RORY sends the email. We hear it go.

AHMED: Another triumphant day!

RORY: Do those work?

AHMED puts down the bowl of paste.

AHMED: It's a show of strength.

INTO:

TOURIST

A non-descript room. Dim natural light only. Tables. Perhaps two or three sewing machines, covered. One still uncovered.

JT enters and surveys the room before indicating for RORY and AHMED to enter.

Standing by the uncovered sewing machine, RANA.

AHMED, carrying a small, cheap video camera.

RORY facing RANA.

RANA: I did invite a student to be in your film but she's gone. Her husband came. Said it was not respectable, on a Friday of all days, a wife should be at home.

RORY: Is there another student you could ask?

RANA: And tell them what? Will we be able to use the machines? Will there be light?

RORY: We brought a generator.

RANA: Fake it, you mean.

AHMED: Rory – I'd be OK to put on a headscarf. If you film me from behind –

RORY: I don't think that's a good idea.

AHMED: We could get some shots of me bent over a machine or something, hide the fact the machine isn't moving –

RORY: Ahmed, that's definitely a bad / idea.

RANA: Look, why not do that for the whole class, just fill it with men dressed as women, let's have a whole world of men, that would certainly solve the respectability problem.

RORY: I know Friday's a bad day, but this funding meeting is in Baghdad on Sunday and I think this film will help us get this gas turbine, which'll double our electricity supply.

RANA: I looked you up. On this 'internet' that we're all getting used to.

RORY: Don't believe everything you read on the internet.

RANA: It says you quit your job at the British Foreign Ministry in order to go walking. It says you walked *six thousand miles*. It says you walked across the mountains of Afghanistan in winter. It says you nearly froze to death.

RORY: Those were the good days.

RANA: So what are we? Your next mountain pass?

RORY: I wouldn't –

RANA: *(Interrupting him.)* You know, Governorate Co-ordinator, for a long time I was a tourist in all this. I only came back to al-Amarah because I thought I should be with my dad during the invasion. And every time when the ministry came to take the machines, or the lights went out, or a husband asked me why after all my sinful years in Baghdad I'm still not married, all through this I kept saying to myself, I don't care, I'll be gone soon, I'm just passing through. And then last week, one of these women, she's never once opened her mouth, she's so meek I find her ridiculous, and last week at the end of class, she waits until everyone else has gone and then she pulls out this piece of work, which she says she cut and stitched herself by hand, secretly, *(RANA shows RORY the piece)* a piece of appliqué. And it's naive of course, but she has, properly, an idea, an idea that is thinking in fabric, and I look at her and her work and the lights that might as well be tubes of milk and I realise I've screwed up, because all the bullshit I wrote to get the money for the course, about how dress-making would develop independent thinking and empower these women out here in the provinces, is coming true. These women are changing. She's the student I asked to come here today. And now I don't know if she'll ever be allowed back.

RORY: Can we interview you, for the film? Say what you just said.

RANA: This new council, what you announced on TV, is that really happening?

RORY: Absolutely.

RANA: My father thinks we're not ready for democracy.

RORY: No one's ever ready.

RANA: Where do you want me to stand?

AHMED: By the machine?

A brief burst of gunfire in the distance.

RANA: Someone's getting married! Firing at the sky to say you're in love. And then every year people at weddings are killed by bullets falling back to earth.

Beat.

RANA: It's a strange thing, sewing. A man does it well, we call him a genius. A woman does it well, we treat her like a servant.

Enter, at the other side of the room, KHALED, with JT.

KHALED walks with a stick. KHALED is in a hurry.

JT: Sorry Rory – this man here says he's her father?

KHALED: Rana, Rana, you need to come home now –

RANA: Baba, I'm working!

KHALED: There's a mob gathering outside the police station –

RORY: What do you mean?

KHALED: Men with guns, swords. From Mu'allimin.

RORY: *(In English, to the soldier.)* Can you find out what's happening?

JT: Comms are busy – We need to get back to the compound, Sir.

RORY: *(To RANA and KHALED.)* I'm just trying to –

RANA: Sorry Baba this is –

KHALED: We saw you on the television. Khaled Bashir. Darling we have to get to the car –

RORY: You're Professor Khaled Bashir? I read your book. Your study of the southern tribes –

KHALED: Really? A reader! That's –

In the distance, from a couple of streets away, we can now hear the chanting of SEYYED HASSAN's congregation gathered outside the police station.

VOICES: Give us Hassan! Give us Hassan! Give us Hassan!

KHALED: Rana, come on – these people are armed! I'm going to start the car.

Exit KHALED.

JT: It's Seyyed Hassan. He's been arrested.

RORY: Arrested for what?

AHMED has gone over to the window to look out.

RANA: They're calling for him.

AHMED: All these men look angry.

KHALED: Another time maybe. Come on Rana –

RORY: Don't go outside until we know –

JT: Seyyed Hassan's congregation are trying to get him out of the police station.

Abu Rashid what? Say again. Over.

Abu Rashid was shot an hour ago. He's dead.

INTO:

ABU RASHID

We hear again the chanting 'Give us Hassan! Give us Hassan!', slowly building in volume.

RORY: *(Out.)* It is the 24th of October, 2003. At the end of Friday prayers, Abu Rashid, the police chief of Maysan province, walks out of Seyyed Hassan's mosque, puts on his shoes, and begins walking down the steps.

We see ABU RASHID exiting the mosque. He looks up and to the right, as if he has seen the shooter.

As he reaches the bottom step, there are two shots. Abu Rashid falls backwards. Blood spreads across his chest.

ABU RASHID puts his hand over his heart, in the traditional Arabic gesture of greeting. He smiles at the audience.

ABU RASHID walks out.

Within an hour, the police have stormed Seyyed Hassan's mosque and seized him. In response his congregation marches on the police station armed with guns and swords.

Where Karim Mahood and the police take up positions on the roof. We can hear them from back in the compound.

We see KARIM with his pistol held above his head.

A single gunshot.

RORY: Don't respond.

A single gunshot.

RORY: It's OK. We can sort this out. Karim just –

RORY is fumbling desperately with his mobile phone, trying to call KARIM –

KARIM: Abu Rashid! Abu Rashid!

RORY: Wait. Wait. Wait.

RORY presses call on the phone.

KARIM: Abu Rashid!

KARIM fires his pistol.

And now, at a suddenly engulfing volume, bursts of automatic gunfire coming from throughout the auditorium –

Deafening noise –

The crowd shouting 'Give us Hassan! Give us Hassan!' Automatic gunfire, screams, shouted orders, a chaos –

And RORY, a still point, cool, thinking hard – he crouches, bows his head, touches the ground –

JT (herself wearing headphones) hands RORY a spare pair of headphones

JT: We're sending in the Warriors sir.

RORY slips on the headphones –

And suddenly the only thing we are hearing is the comms feed for one of the British Army vehicles driving into the middle of the firefight –

COLONEL: *(Speaking into head mic.)* Two Zero Bravo, this is Zero Alpha. Proceed to Blue Eight.

We follow one particular armoured vehicle, a British soldier reporting in –

SOLDIER: *(Distant noise of the gun battle.)* This is Two Zero Bravo in position at Blue Eight. Have sight of police station at Blue Nine. Multiple casualties. Out.

Static hiss.

COLONEL: *(Distant noise of the gun battle, louder.)* Two Zero Bravo, this is Zero Alpha. Proceed to Blue Nine to take up position between attackers and police station. Out.

Static hiss.

SOLDIER: *(Ferocious din as vehicle is now in midst of firefight, ping of bullets and the crump of an RPG hitting the sides of the vehicle.)* This is Two Zero Bravo. Contact. Wait. Out.

Ferocious din builds, supplemented by battle sounds from outside the vehicle –

As RORY stands, hands the phones to JT, springs into action –

INTO:

STATE OF EMERGENCY

A day later.

RORY's office.

RORY has summoned the COLONEL. The COLONEL is wound up tight.

COLONEL: You got what you asked for. Karim has released Seyyed Hassan.

RORY: Good.

COLONEL: Not good. Hassan is bussing in armed supporters Rory. He's getting stronger by the hour.

RORY: We need to talk to both sides.

COLONEL: We need to stop fucking around. We need to go in!

RORY: If you raid Seyyed Hassan's mosque, this city will erupt.

COLONEL: Not if we do it right. Declare a state of emergency –

RORY: Karim was the one who turned the death of Abu Rashid into a crisis by seizing Seyyed Hassan from his mosque in the first place.

COLONEL: Abu Rashid was murdered on the steps of Hassan's mosque. I think that's probable cause.

RORY: He was shot by a sniper from the other side of the street.

COLONEL: You think Hassan couldn't arrange that?

RORY: I'm saying it could have been anyone. The Iranians. Drug smugglers. If Seyyed Hassan wanted to kill Abu Rashid why do it right outside his own mosque?

COLONEL: Why not? You know he'll be unarmed because he's going to Friday prayers. You have backup at ground level because you control the mosque. And you have ample time to prepare because the Governorate Co-ordinator arranged the fucking visit.

Beat.

COLONEL: Was it Seyyed Hassan's idea, that Abu Rashid go to Friday prayers?

RORY: It was.

COLONEL: And was it not one of Seyyed Hassan's congregation who told you some cock-and-bull story about an Abu Ali – which is basically the commonest name imaginable, right?

RORY: I'm sure he was telling the truth –

COLONEL: And on that basis you let Abu Rashid walk undefended into a fucking snake pit.

RORY: Abu Rashid understood that to do his job effectively, at some point he was going to have to talk to Seyyed Hassan.

COLONEL: Abu Rashid went to see Seyyed Hassan because he liked you, Rory, and because he was reckless and because he was impressed, as we all were, that you'd done your job and unblocked whatever blockage it was in Baghdad and got the money for his men.

RORY: Baghdad hasn't actually released the salaries for the police.

COLONEL: But you paid them?

RORY: I took the money from a canal rebuilding project. I was hoping the money would come through from Baghdad before it was…discovered.

Beat.

COLONEL: Listen, Rory. Hassan has played you. That's clear enough. Now's your chance to roll this back. Show Seyyed Hassan your authority. Postpone the Council.

RORY: I've already announced it.

COLONEL: Now is not the time.

RORY: We cannot continue to rule through one man.

COLONEL: Karim Mahood has made this province work for us. He's our friend.

RORY: We didn't come here to install a tribal warlord.

COLONEL: He's not a warlord!

RORY: People won't accept it.

COLONEL: They were accepting it until you arrived.

Beat.

RORY: It's what we've always done. Find our Prince, our Rajah. But we've come here promising something different. For the first time, we've said it has to be democracy.

COLONEL: These people don't want democracy. They want to be not fucking dead.

A phone call from SEYYED HASSAN.

HASSAN: Governorate Co-ordinator. Friend. Karim's men have taken my brother. He's been taken hostage. He is my youngest brother. They pulled him out of school. He's fifteen years old.

INTO:

OCCUPATIONAL HAZARDS: ACT ONE

THESIGER

RORY's office. 24 hours later.

RANA has brought her father KHALED around to help RORY talk through the escalating crisis.

RORY: You know more about the southern tribes than anyone.

KHALED: Book learning –

RORY: I need your advice. Maysan needs your advice.

KHALED: In my life in Iraq I've learned to avoid politics.

RANA: Baba.

RORY: Politics has come to you.

KHALED: I'm not a brave man. I'm an academic.

RORY: There are armed men filling the streets.

RANA: We've seen them. Baba.

KHALED: In Iraq, brave men lead short lives.

RANA: Baba.

   Beat.

KHALED: Explain it to me.

RORY: It's about the law of blood.

KHALED: I expected that.

RORY: Karim Mahood says he'll release Seyyed Hassan's brother if Seyyed Hassan hands over a Doctor Latif.

KHALED: And this Doctor Latif is…

RORY: Who Karim now says killed Abu Rashid.

KHALED: Is Karim right to suspect this Dr Latif?

RORY: Parts of a sniper rifle were found at this Dr Latif's house this morning. But as it was Karim's men who organised the raid –

RANA: You think Karim planted these weapons to incriminate Latif?

RORY: Exactly. The question is, Professor, if I can speak to Karim and if we promise that the British Army will investigate this Dr Latif, would Karim's tribe be willing to release Seyyed Hassan's brother?

KHALED: The murder of Abu Rashid was too blatant.

RORY: Then could Latif's tribe pay blood money?

KHALED: Only by admitting their guilt. If Karim's tribe fail to avenge Abu Rashid's murder, they make themselves weak. If Seyyed Hassan gives up Doctor Latif he makes himself weak. This is Iraq. This is a country where a ruler pretends to have weapons he does not have, even if by doing so, he brings on his own destruction.

RORY: You're saying there's no way out?

KHALED: Send in the tanks! Crush Seyyed Hassan and the Sadrists while you still have the chance.

RORY: That's your best answer?

KHALED: I'm a historian! I don't take the decision. I only point out afterwards how it went wrong. I was born facing backwards. You know the line from Walter Benjamin? The angel of history, hurtling into the future, facing backwards? There are no heroes, Rory.

Beat.

RORY: Thesiger.

RANA: Thesiger? Who's Thesiger?

KHALED: An eccentric British primitivist!

RORY: He negotiates a truce in a blood feud – to save a friend –

KHALED: That was fifty years ago –

RORY: But it shows it can be done. An outsider, a neutral figure –

KHALED: Thesiger had lived amongst those tribes for years.

RORY: But if it was a gathering –

RANA: I've heard you talk about things like that –

RORY: Sheikh of Sheikhs – wasn't that it? I've read that somewhere –

KHALED: In my damned book!

RANA: You were saying last night the answer had to come from the tribes.

KHALED: That was Johnny Walker talking! He's got me into trouble before.

RORY: Make it bigger. A summit, invite everyone, the tribes the political parties, the clerics –

KHALED: Rory, you're not an Iraqi. This will seem arrogant, vain, dangerous.

Beat.

RORY: We'll call it for tomorrow night.

KHALED: Oh God!

RORY goes to the door of the office.

RORY: Ahmed! Can you gather all the translators and the political team? They're going to be making a lot of calls.

Back to the room.

KHALED: Rana.

RORY: We'll need somewhere bigger than the Council building.

RANA: You could use the theatre. Nothing interesting's happened there for ages.

RORY: Perfect. You two must come?

KHALED: Rory, we're leaving al-Amarah. We have some deliveries to make for the museum and then we're gone. My daughter only persuaded me to come because, well, you've met her.

KHALED looks at his watch.

KHALED: Darling, we have to be gone before dark.

RANA: Give me a minute.

KHALED: You have this new portable phone, Rana?

RORY: Thank you for coming, Professor.

KHALED: May God shield you, Governorate Co-ordinator.

Exit KHALED.

RORY: What did he mean, 'deliveries'?

RANA: We're clearing out the museum.

RORY: You're not serious?

RANA: The most valuable artefacts. We're smuggling them out one by one in our bags.

RORY: You have something in there?

RANA: *(Nods.)* Sometimes if you do something unbelievably stupid, it works, because nobody believes you would do it.

RORY: That seems to be one of my principles in life.

RANA pulls a padded envelope out of her handbag.

RANA: This is the oldest clay tablet we have.

RORY: Can I…?

RANA hands RORY the envelope.

RORY pulls a small wooden box, about the size of a large matchbox, out of the padded envelope.

RANA: Five thousand years old.

He unlatches it, pulls away a top layer of padding.

He touches the surface of the clay tablet.

RANA: I don't think you're supposed to do that.

RORY: What do you think will be left of us in five thousand years?

RANA: Not much at this rate.

AHMED comes in.

AHMED: The political team are ready. Who should we call first?

RORY: I'll be through in a moment.

AHMED exits.

RORY: My father always says: stop making decisions and you're dead. If you wait too long, people start to think you aren't going to deliver. Better to do something, find out if it works…

RANA: We'll be there, at the meeting. My dad can have the car outside. With the engine running, if need be. My dad is always saying, this can't be done, it's impossible. It's the one thing he'll never learn – the impossible happens all the time.

INTO:

THE GREEN ROOM

The next day.

In the theatre building. A 'green room' area/dressing room.

The hubbub of an audience from nearby.

RORY, AHMED and JT.

RORY: They all in?

AHMED: Karim's just parking his Toyota.

RORY: The Colonel?

JT: He's here. He's got Basrah standing by to send reinforcements. If this meeting doesn't work.

Exit JT.

AHMED: Remember Rory: "This is the true joy in life, the being used for a purpose recognized by yourself as a mighty one…the being a force of nature instead of a feverish, selfish little clod of ailments and grievances complaining that the world will not devote itself to making you happy." Mister George Bernard Shaw

Exit AHMED.

RORY looks for a moment at a small sheet of paper, then puts it away in his jacket pocket. Straightens his tie.

RORY: *(Out.)* Stop making decisions and you're dead. Stop making decisions and you're dead. Stop making decisions –

INTO:

SHEIKH OF SHEIKHS

The theatre in al-Amarah. Bare stage with chairs set up for this meeting.

House lights up, somewhat, on the audience, to represent the gathered notables of al-Amarah.

RORY is centre stage.

On a chair to one side, SEYYED HASSAN.

On a chair facing, KARIM MAHOOD, wearing an even grander tribal robe than before, and carrying a black plastic bag.

Also present, as if in the audience – RANA, KHALED, RIFAT, MUSAB, AHMED, JT and the COLONEL.

A cameraman from Maysan TV is holding a camera, filming the meeting.

RORY addresses the assembly, characters and audience members. As he names each group he looks at them, establishes eye contact.

RORY: Leaders of al-Amarah. Tribal sheikhs, religious and political leaders, leaders of the unions, businesses, NGOs. Karim Mahood. Colonel. Peace be upon you. The events of the last days have been a tragedy for this great province. This is a famous province, a province which liberated itself. This province will have soon its own Council and elect its own governor. All this is fragile. Tonight you need to decide, if you are going to live by rules, or descend into endless war. Who would like to speak first?

SEYYED HASSAN puts up his hand.

RORY: Seyyed Hassan.

HASSAN: In the name of God, the compassionate, the merciful, praise to God, the Lord of the worlds. I stand before you as a man of peace.

KARIM: *(Scoffs.)*

HASSAN: The men who kidnapped me, the men who assaulted my body are here in this room. My brother, who is still a child, has been taken. I don't know where he is or –

KARIM: Then give us Doctor Latif!

RORY: Karim! *(To SEYYED HASSAN.)* We regret the way you and your family have been treated. We deplore it.

RIFAT: It's a crime!

MUSAB: *(Calming.)* Brother!

RORY: But the police need to talk to Doctor Latif. Weapons were found at his house, Seyyed. Witnesses have spoken of him.

HASSAN: Doctor Latif was in Najaf on Friday! He had nothing to do with the death of Abu Rashid.

RORY: It would be better, Seyyed, if Doctor Latif could explain himself directly to the police.

HASSAN: So you reward Karim Mahood's hostage-taking?

RORY: No. But we need to find Abu Rashid's killer. Through the law.

HASSAN: And how will these police treat Doctor Latif? Will they beat him? Will they threaten his life?

RIFAT: This is crusader justice!

MUSAB: Rifat, please.

HASSAN: Karim Mahood has killed members of my congregation –

RORY: They were attacking the police station.

HASSAN: They were trying to rescue me.

RORY: RPGs were fired. When you fire guns in the centre of the city.

HASSAN: I had been kidnapped! I was bound to a chair!

RORY: You created the conditions for their actions, Seyyed. You spoke violence in your sermons. And your followers are out on the streets of this city now.

HASSAN: *(Gestures to RIFAT, MUSAB.)* My followers are aflame with anger! If they want to defend me, what can I do?

RORY: You can say something. Your words have power. That's why you're here. That's why we're all here.

HASSAN: If you want to know the murderer of Abu Rashid, I will point him out for you. *(Pointing at the COLONEL.)* The British Colonel!

RORY: Don't be ridiculous.

HASSAN: The reckless policy of the British Colonel led to the violence on Friday and you know it.

RORY: The Colonel and his men risked their lives, driving their vehicles between your supporters and the police station.

KARIM: This is disgusting!

HASSAN: The Colonel has deliberately ignored the religious parties and carried out every wish of his friend the criminal Mahood –

RORY: If the British Army had not acted on Friday, you would have destroyed this city. You're speaking like a child.

HASSAN: This is colonialist arrogance!

RORY: *(Angrily.)* No, Seyyed. My father served as a colonial officer. My grandfather was a colonial officer. We could have come here to build a colony but we're not doing that. We came here to transfer power to you. We want to return home.

KARIM: You see Colonel! The Sadr Office wants to attack you. If you won't attack them, I will.

COLONEL: I understand your anger, Karim –

RORY: *(Cutting him off.)* You have no authority to take armed men into the streets, Karim. Anyone who does so may be fired on by British troops.

KARIM: Have you not been listening? This man is your enemy.

RORY: My enemy is chaos. I thought we shared that enemy.

KARIM: My police will arrest Hassan a second time.

RORY: Your police must behave according to the law.

KARIM: Taking hostages is the tribal way.

RORY: When your men put on their police uniforms, they take on a sacred duty.

KARIM: And when you trick them? With money from some canal builder? When you lie to Abu Rashid to send him to his death? What sacred duty is that?

RORY: That was a misunderstanding.

HASSAN: What are you talking about?

KARIM: What are you? All lies and empty promises?

KHALED: Excuse me. Professor Khaled Bashir. University of al-Amarah. Karim Mahood, when you use tribal methods you forget that the men you attack also have tribes and they will be forced to take vengeance on you. That is all.

HASSAN turns on KARIM.

HASSAN: You see! Learned men speak against you. You are a disgrace to your friend Abu Rashid –

KARIM: Say nothing of Abu Rashid –

HASSAN: You have no right to his blood –

KARIM: Abu Rashid was a great man!

HASSAN: You are less than his shadow –

Suddenly KARIM has reached into his plastic bag and pulled out ABU RASHID's shirt, covered in dried blood, with two tightly grouped bullet holes in the chest (and larger exit holes in the back.).

KARIM: This is the blood of Abu Rashid!

RORY: Karim – this has to stop –

HASSAN stands and recoils from this horror.

HASSAN: See how the tribes want to drag us into the past!

KARIM: Abu Rashid's blood cries out for vengeance!

RORY: We have come here to replace vengeance –

KARIM: This is the blood of Abu Rashid!

KARIM has stepped over towards SEYYED HASSAN and has thrust the bloodied shirt into HASSAN's face.

RORY: Karim – stop now!

KARIM: And now your brother must pay!

HASSAN: I will never give you Doctor Latif. Doctor Latif is an associate of our leader Moqtada –

KARIM: Moqtada is a fool –

COLONEL: For God's sake, Karim! You need to put that away now.

RIFAT: We defend Hassan! *(Repeats this.)*

HASSAN: What did you say?

MUSAB: For the sake of God, Rifat!

KARIM: Moqtada is wrong in the head –

HASSAN: Moqtada is the son of our founder –

RORY: Karim – Seyyed –

KARIM: He's a fanatic–

HASSAN: Moqtada is close to God!

KARIM: Ranting like an idiot –

And just as JT and another SOLDIER are about to step in –

AHMED has stood up.

He sings over the top of KARIM and HASSAN's fury.

AHMED: *(Slowly singing, building from a low volume.)* Blessed be God, Mohammed and Ali Mohammed.

HASSAN: You dare not speak of Moqtada!

KARIM: I speak for the blood of Abu Rashid! This is the blood of Abu Rashid!

HASSAN and the others have stopped mid-sentence.

AHMED: *(Repeating.)* Blessed be God, Mohammed and Ali Mohammed.

Now KARIM stops too.

All present, apart from RORY and the COLONEL, but most especially KARIM and HASSAN, join in.

ALL IN UNISON: *(Singing.)* Blessed be God, Mohammed and Ali Mohammed. God bless Mohammed and the children of Mohammed.

Beat.

AHMED: Seyyed. Sheikh. Please, be seated.

SEYYED HASSAN and KARIM sit back down.

RORY: Thank you.

AHMED sits down.

RORY: Not far from this building lie the remains of the world's first civilisation: clay tablets covered in an alphabet invented here five thousand years ago, eighty-five generations before anyone in Britain or America began to write.

RORY pulls a small box out of his pocket (the box we saw earlier), removes the lid and holds up the box so that everyone can see.

RORY: This is one of those clay tablets. From your museum, here in al-Amarah. And what did your ancestors do when they had invented writing? What did they write on these tablets of wet clay, using reeds cut from the marshes? They wrote laws. Five thousand years ago, when the people of my country were living in chaos, your ancestors invented the law.

Now you have a choice. Today I'm going to ask you all to sign a document committing you and the people you speak for to respect the rule of law. You, as leaders, will promise to control your followers, and when they break the law not to punish them yourselves, but to hand them over to the police.

Karim Mahood. Seyyed Hassan. You have never met before today. You both fought bravely against Saddam. You both have your martyrs. Look at each other. Look now.

The two men look at each other.

HASSAN: I cannot entrust Doctor Latif to this man.

RORY: If you like, Seyyed, instead of the police, the British Army can take Doctor Latif into custody.

KARIM throws his arms up in disgust.

HASSAN: When my brother is released, Doctor Latif will present himself to you, for questioning.

RORY: I will take him.

KARIM: This is a betrayal!

KARIM stands up to go.

RORY: Karim. Wait. You and Abu Rashid and your men lived for many years as outlaws, fighting bravely against Saddam. Everyone here knows that. But the outlaw days are passing. Now is the time for government, for steady building. Abu Rashid understood. Democracy is coming. This is not against the tribes, Karim. This meeting is the inheritance of the tribes.

KARIM looks from SEYYED HASSAN to RORY. He looks at the other people in the meeting – and at the audience.

The cameraman has taken a couple of steps forward, and, for the first time, KARIM has remembered he is on camera.

KARIM: Abu Rashid could name a hundred different kinds of bird. His wife is now a widow and his children fatherless. He was the first police chief of our free al-Amarah. He was cut down like a tree. The Albu Muhammad agree not to pursue the blood feud for his murder. Let the British Army investigate. I will release Seyyed Hassan's brother in return for Doctor Latif. And I will be the first to sign your document, to commit myself and my followers to the rule of law. I, Karim, son of Mahood, son of Hattab, of the Albu Muhammad, the greatest tribe of the south.

End of Act One

Act Two

MARMALADE

RORY's office.

The next day.

A moment alone, a moment to breathe.

RORY smiles at the audience.

RORY: *(Out.)* What was that? Politics or theatre?

The COLONEL breezes in with JT.

COLONEL: Good Morning Rory.

RORY: Morning.

COLONEL: Got the bastards. Whole gang by the look of it. Had a couple of tonnes of copper wire under a tarp.

RORY: *(To the COLONEL.)* So Seyyed Hassan was helpful in finding them?

COLONEL: Yes, he was.

Enter AHMED carrying a plate of oatcakes with marmalade on them.

AHMED: Rory, Colonel, I thought, as today is our first day of interviews for the Council, and as we are celebrating that we are not all dead, we should have some of the special top quality marmalade kindly sent by Mrs Stewart. On the oatcakes also the gift of Mrs Stewart.

JT hands RORY a short (10-20cm) length of copper wire.

JT: Thought you'd like a souvenir sir. Spoils of war.

RORY: I'll add it to my collection.

JT: If we can just get that bloody turbine then we can really get the bloody lights on. Sir.

COLONEL makes to leave. Stops.

COLONEL: Your summit meeting last night– whatever you called it – Sheikh of Sheikhs! That was a bloody good show. I didn't believe you could do it.

RORY: You made that very clear, Colonel.

COLONEL: Well, we learn.

RORY: Are we ready to go?

AHMED: There are people waiting to get into the waiting room for the waiting room.

COLONEL: Everyone wants to be on your Council!

COLONEL and JT breeze out.

RORY: In the meeting, when you calmed the room –

AHMED: I told you: I don't like arguing!

RORY: No but why the prayer? Why did you use the prayer?

AHMED: I wanted to say I too am a Muslim. This also is Islam.

RORY: You saved us.

AHMED: It was nothing compared to your fine words. 'The Outlaw Days are passing.' I mean: what was that?

RORY: I don't know I was – improvising –

AHMED: It was hilarious.

RORY: I was bored. Back in Scotland, before I came here. Worse than bored. I was numb. Not fully alive.

AHMED: Of course! And now you have the 'true joy'. *(Beat.)* You were great. In the meeting.

RORY: Thank you.

AHMED does not leave.

RORY: Ahmed, would you like an oatcake?

AHMED: Well…

AHMED takes an oatcake.

Enter KARIM –

KARIM: I said I would be the first and here I am.

AHMED gives a pained smile.

RORY: *(Out.)* Interview Number One –

KARIM: You will announce the Council in six weeks?

RORY: The plan hasn't changed Karim. Forty councillors –

KARIM: And then these forty will elect the Governor.

RORY: That's right. Marmalade, Karim? It's a British delicacy.

KARIM: This is full of sugar.

KARIM brings out a sheet of paper with a long list of names on it on both sides.

KARIM: I need tell you nothing more about myself. But I have brought you a list of good men from the tribes.

RORY: This is a long list.

KARIM: These are important tribes. Will you be talking to Seyyed Hassan?

RORY: Seyyed Hassan is helping us.

KARIM: Seyyed Hassan is not your friend.

RORY: You made peace.

KARIM: Yes! We made peace.

RORY: *(Out.)* And so it begins – every day, a dozen meetings – sheikhs and judges, clerics and mayors –

Time passes.

AHMED enters again with a fresh plate of oatcakes and marmalade.

RORY: How many is that?

AHMED: Interview number forty-eight!

RORY: *(Out.)* Baghdad won't let us hold an election. Partly they say because we're not ready, partly because they say that 'early elections lead to domination by extremist parties'.

Good Morning Gentlemen.

Enter SEYYED HASSAN and RIFAT. RIFAT is much more smartly dressed than before.

HASSAN: Thank you for agreeing to meet my colleague, Rifat.

RORY: We've met before. How is your brother?

RIFAT: Completely healed.

HASSAN: Rifat has begun to work at my mosque, helping with the distribution of food parcels.

RIFAT: We are sorry for September the eleventh.

RORY: You really don't need to apologise for that.

RIFAT: It was the work of Sunni madmen.

RORY: The house of Islam has many rooms.

RIFAT: Exactly! And some of those rooms should be locked and then we break the key. Seyyed Hassan has taught me to govern my anger. Now I wish we can work together, bringing food, jobs…

Time passes.

AHMED comes in again with a fresh plate of oatcakes and marmalade.

RORY: *(Out.)* After the first one hundred and fifty interviews, I put up the leading names on a board and move them back and forth, off and on, balancing different factions, warring tribes, like the seating plan at the world's most awkward wedding…

During this, RORY has unveiled said board –

AHMED takes an oatcake with marmalade. Munches absent-mindedly while looking at the board. Exhales.

AHMED: At this wedding, half the guests are clerics.

RORY: It's a work in progress –

AHMED: When you choose the Council then, really, you choose who is elected Governor.

RORY: It's not as predictable as that –

AHMED: But if you choose *this* Council –

RORY: Well, yes. It's a guiding hand.

Beat.

AHMED: You heard the Christians have gone.

RORY: What do you mean, gone? All of them?

AHMED: The family that sold alcohol, on Dijla Street. They've gone to Damascus.

Beat.

Pause. AHMED goes to leave, then picks up a second oatcake with marmalade and eats it.

RORY covers up the board –

Enter SEYYED HASSAN and RIFAT.

RORY: Your followers were harassing the Christian family that sold alcohol on Dijla Street.

RIFAT: Alcohol is forbidden.

RORY: There's no law in Iraq against alcohol.

RIFAT: This is a Muslim country!

RORY: There have been Christians here for centuries.

HASSAN: Rifat. Rory. The men involved in this incident were acting without my knowledge.

RORY: You need to control your followers.

HASSAN: Their passion outstripped their wisdom. I've spoken to them.

RIFAT: Exactly. What he said.

HASSAN: We disagree on some fundamental things, Governorate Co-ordinator. But we understand each other. We have met well, praise to God. Have we not?

SEYYED HASSAN holds out his hand for RORY to shake.

RORY shakes SEYYED HASSAN's hand.

Time passes.

AHMED rushes in with another plate of oatcakes and marmalade.

AHMED: Rory! We need the list. For Maysan TV.

RORY: *(Out.)* Interviews completed. Two hundred and twenty-three.

AHMED: The presenter is calling up every five minutes.

KARIM rushes in with his new idea –

KARIM: Mister Rory, how many minorities do you have on the Council?

RORY: It's done, Karim –

KARIM: The religious minorities: Christians, Sunni, Sabian Mandaeans. The Council should have one of each.

RORY: But there are no more than a few families from each of those groups.

KARIM: All the more important to protect them. We need a Council based on human rights. Human rights means protecting minorities. You believe in human rights, don't you?

RORY: I've never heard you mention them.

KARIM: I'm learning from you. And women. We need plenty of women. Women are…great. Mothers. Daughters. Sisters. Al-Amarah needs women.

RORY: You expect these women and religious minorities will vote for you as Governor?

KARIM: It's a question of principle.

RORY: The tribes are very well represented on the Council, I can assure –

KARIM: Do you not see what Seyyed Hassan is doing? The Christians on Dijla Street –

RORY: I've spoken to him about that –

KARIM: They've already closed the video shops, the guitar seller, the internet café – we only just got the internet!

RORY: I'm sorry Karim –

AHMED comes in with the satphone –

AHMED: It's Baghdad –

RORY: *(To KARIM.)* Excuse me –

BREMER in the Green Zone, on the phone to RORY.

BREMER: Hey Rory. I hear you're announcing your Council. Just wanted to say: We did not invade Iraq to turn it into Iran.

RORY: Have you been speaking to Karim?

BREMER: We read your sitrep! A 'more inclusive approach'! At first reading, we liked the sound of that. Then we wondered: what does that mean?

RORY: It means bringing the most powerful groups in the province into government.

BREMER: Look, Rory, I believe in the lost art of delegation. You do what you think is right. But you've walked through Iran. You've seen the secret police in every village.

RORY: We need to reflect this world –

BREMER: We're making this world. To simply reflect, too late for that, don't you think?

RORY ends the call –

KARIM: Was that Jerry?

Enter JT –

JT: Rory –

RORY: Is transport ready for the studio?

JT: It's not that. It's the sewing class.

INTO:

THE CANDIDATE

The living room of RANA and KHALED's house in the nicer part of al-Amarah. A well furnished, educated, bourgeois Iraqi home.

RORY has just arrived.

KHALED is carrying an open bottle of Johnny Walker and a glass. He is distressed and a little drunk.

RANA is wearing an 'indoors' headscarf and a modest dress.

KHALED: You shouldn't have come Rory. There's nothing to say.

RORY: *(To RANA.)* What happened?

KHALED: Young men, Rory. They say things they don't mean. They show off.

RORY: Are you hurt?

RANA: They broke three of the machines.

RORY: You're sure they were Sadrists?

RANA: Of course I'm sure.

KHALED: They only got their beards last week. They don't know how to behave.

RANA: They said I needed disciplining.

KHALED: That's enough, Rana.

RANA: One of them –

KHALED: Don't say these things! When you say things, you lose control of them. They are out in the world.

Beat: RANA stops herself from saying something.

RORY: I'm going to speak to Seyyed Hassan.

KHALED: For God's sake don't draw more attention to us, please. Thank you for coming Rory. You're a busy man. You need to get to the Television Studio. We will carry on. Everything will carry on.

Beat.

KHALED: I should be drinking more slowly as it's the last fucking bottle of Johnny Walker in al-Amarah.

RANA: How many Sadrists have you chosen for the Council?

KHALED: Leave him alone, Rana.

RORY: I'll be announcing that in a couple of hours.

RANA: No harm in telling me now then.

RORY: Eight.

RANA: Eight? Including Seyyed Hassan?

RORY: Yes.

RANA: And from the other religious parties?

RORY: Another twelve.

RANA: Meaning twenty out of forty are from the religious parties?

RORY: They're significant / figures –

RANA: So if Seyyed Hassan stands for governor, he'll get it –

KHALED: We will live, no matter what.

RANA: I want to know.

KHALED sits down, nurses his Scotch.

RANA: And the ordinary people? The lawyers, the doctors?

RORY: We have a lawyer, a trades unionist. But very few have come forward –

RANA: And women?

RORY: Two. Of five who applied.

RANA: I went to nightclubs in Baghdad, Rory. I wore skirts to the knee.

RORY: This is the south. Women dress differently here –

RANA: You're lecturing me on how the women of al-Amarah dress?

RORY: No I –

RANA: What you're seeing now – this is already worse. When I came here from Baghdad before the invasion, I could still wear a coloured hijab, a decent coat – now look! It's a sea of black. *(Angrily tugs on her abaya – a shapeless black cloak.)* Swallowing up our oh so shameful bodies –

KHALED: Rana!

RANA: At the university, the Sadrist students are already agitating for segregated classes.

RORY: I didn't – [know that]

RANA looks to KHALED.

KHALED: It's true. Pre-Islamic history will be the next thing to go –

RORY: Seyyed Hassan wouldn't agree to that. He's not anti-intellectual.

RANA: He's anti-everything since the death of the Prophet!

RORY: He's an engineer!

RANA: So he's a thug with a degree!

RORY: If Seyyed Hassan hadn't believed I was serious about sharing power, we would never have made peace.

RANA: You're saying, you have to include Seyyed Hassan, or he'll send his people back out onto the streets? Which is it? He's a great engineer, or he's got a gun to your head?

KHALED: It's not that simple.

RANA: Seyyed Hassan doesn't even want democracy! He thinks it's against God's will.

RORY: No one wants democracy. They want power for their people. Democracy is what prevents them getting too much of it.

RANA: You appoint a council like this, it sends a message into every mosque, every school –

RORY: Have you ever thought that the people of al-Amarah might want Seyyed Hassan?

RANA: This is a modern country, Rory!

RORY: He has support!

RANA: From a tiny number of poor, illiterate, lied-to people.

KHALED: We don't know that.

RANA: You admire him, don't you?

RORY: It doesn't matter what I feel.

RANA: Like those men you met on your walk across Afghanistan.

RORY: I have to get on.

RANA: On to the next mountain pass? Put Seyyed Hassan in charge of Maysan and keep on walking?

RORY: Don't be ridiculous.

RANA: I've fought to control my life. I turned down the man my parents wanted me to marry. I set up my business in Baghdad.

RORY: I have to bring the Sadrists into government.

RANA: You came to my class Rory. You saw what's happening in those women's *minds.*

RORY: We need these men.

RANA: How they're seeing themselves as makers, as creators. You were moved, listening to them. I saw it in your face.

RORY: Your class means nothing! It's a handful of lucky people in a province of a million. A province of tribes and religion and power.

Beat.

RORY: You complain there are so few secular candidates. Then why aren't you standing? Why aren't you?

Beat.

RORY: I should go.

KHALED: You should. Thank you Rory.

RORY: I'll get new sewing machines.

RANA: They said I should be raped.

KHALED: Rana. This is shameful.

RANA: The men who came to the class. They held me against the wall. Said I was a whore. Said I should be disciplined like a whore. Said that Seyyed Hassan had talked about my class in his sermon.

Beat.

RANA: You cannot have democracy at the ballot box so long as you have tyranny in the home.

RORY: I'm sorry. I shouldn't have said what I said about –

RANA: No, you spoke the truth.

RORY: I was speaking without –

RANA: No, you're right. The class is just a beginning.

KHALED: The class is more than enough.

RANA: Why aren't people like me standing?

KHALED: This is madness.

RANA: We have this opportunity. We're free. And now we have to fight to defend that.

KHALED: Rana, as your father, who loves you and protects you, I forbid you to say a word more.

RANA: I want you to interview me for the Council.

RORY: You want to stand?

KHALED: God in heaven!

RORY: We can't provide security. Given what's happened –

RANA: You think I shouldn't stand?

KHALED: Please stop this!

RANA: If we don't speak, then who will speak for us?

KHALED: Rory, you've seen the world. My daughter does not know where she is.

RANA: I know exactly where I am.

KHALED: We're hollow men! The years of Saddam have hollowed us out. Look at our streets full of preachers and thugs.

RANA: People learn, people change.

KHALED: People are stones! We can no more make a democracy than I could grow horns. Not in a hundred years. Rory, my friend, will you please stop my daughter doing this foolish thing?

Pause.

RORY: Rana's a strong candidate. And I'm reducing the number of Islamists on the Council.

INTO:

THE BIRTH OF DEMOCRACY

A dingy committee room, the windows dusty and crossed with bomb tape.

From outside, the noise of a crowd of Sadrist protesters: 'Council of Lies! Council of Lies!', 'Down with Crusaders!'

Seated around a square of tables, the new Council of al-Amarah. (Again, if the audience can in some way feel included in this gathering, all to the good.)

At the centre, RORY.

The Council is electing the new Iraqi Governor for Maysan.

Present around the table, KARIM, RANA, RIFAT and SEYYED HASSAN. Others – Abu Ivan, Ali Hammod, other tribal and religious leaders – may also be represented. Seated elsewhere, the COLONEL.

Standing to one side of RORY, AHMED.

RORY: Men and women of the Council, I'm honoured to have participated in your first act, to elect a Governor of this great province.

AHMED hands RORY a folded sheet of paper, which RORY opens

RORY: And we have a result. Abu Ivan, Communist Party of al-Amarah, three votes. Seyyed Hassan, Office of Muqtada al-Sadr, sixteen votes –

KARIM: This is a fraud! This vote is –

RORY: Ali Hammod, Independent, four votes.

KARIM: This vote is a conspiracy –

RORY: Karim Mahood, Sheikh of the Albu Muhammad, seventeen votes. I therefore declare that Karim Mahood is elected the first democratic governor of al-Amarah.

KARIM: We need a rec [ount] – What / I've won.

HASSAN: If the Governorate Co-ordinator had not excluded four of my followers, the result would have been different.

RIFAT: It's crusader democracy!

Abu Ivan or Ali Hammod, if represented, concede in a couple of words here.

KARIM: I'm governor. Of course I am. Good.

The COLONEL comes over to congratulate KARIM.

KARIM embraces him, with some panache.

If KARIM's allies are represented, he may embrace one or two of them, in a swirl of excitement.

Then he turns to RORY.

RORY: Congratulations.

RORY holds out his hand to KARIM.

For a moment KARIM will not shake RORY's hand.

Then he does so.

RORY: Welcome to government.

KARIM: I won.

RORY steps aside, and KARIM takes his place.

KARIM: So. People of Maysan. Arabs! Proud Iraqi Arabs. We have waited for many months while the British and the Americans dither and fumble. Now finally we can begin! I have lived in this province all my life, except for my time in Abu Ghraib. I understand the ways of the tribes. I fear God, but I'm not a fanatic. I have been to school, but not too much.

A long beat.

KARIM: Two days ago, the impossible happened. They found him! Cowering like a rat in a hole!

Beat.

KARIM: Saddam can never come back. Tell your children. Fear is abolished. I'm now your governor. The Governor of al-Amarah. The most beautiful city in the world.

KARIM sits down.

Pause: we can hear the chanting outside.

RORY: You can carry on Karim.

KARIM stands up.

KARIM: My first act as governor. The followers of Seyyed Hassan have chosen to stand outside the Council building, shouting unacceptable insults. We need to clear the square.

HASSAN: My followers are expressing their anger at the anti-Islamic prejudice of the British Government.

KARIM: Your followers can express their anger at our tanks.

COLONEL: Karim, the British Army controls security. It will operate according to the law. You do not have the authority to order British tanks into the square.

Beat.

RORY: *(Pointing to the table.)* Perhaps the agenda?

KARIM looks down and sees the sheet in front of him.

KARIM: Right. The first thing is… We have received more money to employ the young men of the city. Good. I've been asking for this for months. We will take this money and add it to the current scheme.

RIFAT: Where you give all the jobs to your tribe?

KARIM: We give jobs to the men who need them –

RIFAT: You have no idea who needs them.

HASSAN: We at the Sadr Office know who needs these jobs most.

KARIM: I will supply Rory with a list of names.

RIFAT: We need an independent list.

KARIM: As the elected governor I will issue a decree to spend this money.

HASSAN: Already you pervert your office.

KARIM: The members of the Council have just elected me.

RORY: Actually Karim, the governor requires a vote of the Council for spending of this size.

KARIM: The Council just voted for me.

RORY: It was agreed before you were elected, all spending above the level of twenty thousand dollars needs Council approval. You all need to agree.

KARIM looks around the room at the members of the Provincial Council.

KARIM: We need to agree? We forty?

RORY: You need a majority.

KARIM looks around the room in horror.

Beat.

KARIM: As the duly elected governor of Maysan Province, I move that the Sadrist members of this Council should be expelled immediately –

Uproar.

INTO:

THE CROWD (ONE)

The street outside the Council building.

MUSAB rallies the crowd, perhaps carrying a large green flag with white Arabic script on it. He is now wearing a 'Nikey' knock-off baseball cap.

MUSAB: Down with the Council of Lies! Down with the Council of Lies! Down with Crooked Mahood! Down with Crooked Mahood! Seyyed Hassan for Governor! Seyyed Hassan for Governor!

INTO:

CLEARING THE SQUARE

RORY's office –

KARIM and RORY

RORY: You can't expel Seyyed Hassan from the Council –

KARIM: Have you seen what he's writing?

RORY: Ignore it –

KARIM: He says I've given all the jobs and building contracts to my friends.

RORY: Right. Well – let's talk about the next phase of refurbishing the schools –

KARIM: *(Reading.)* 'Now we see how Crooked Mahood and his illegal Council rape the people of al-Amarah –'

RORY: OK that is bad –

KARIM: It's Sadrist filth!

RORY: The Education Director has produced an excellent – [plan].

KARIM: *(Reads further.)* 'Now we see the true nature of the Hitler Rory Stewart –'

RORY: Hitler? That's new.

KARIM: *(Ignoring this.)* 'Now we see the results of this unholy Jewish conspiracy –'

RORY: They're going to have to choose between that and the Hitler.

KARIM: Do you think this is funny?

RORY: No, I –

KARIM: How am I meant to command respect when the paper is printing this slander? We need to clear the square.

RORY: If we do that, there'll be bloodshed. Let me talk to the protesters.

KARIM: We need to send in the tanks. That's what people respect.

RORY: Karim. I know this is difficult. But it will get better. When the gas turbine I told you about is delivered –

KARIM: When? When?

RORY: Next month. And when it comes you make a TV broadcast in front of it, your first big speech as governor. 'I, Karim Mahood, am delivering for you, the people of Maysan.'

KARIM: I've had nothing to do with the turbine.

RORY: You'll be blamed for a thousand things you can't control. So when something good happens, take credit for it. Once you've shown people what you can do, it will get better.

INTO:

THE CROWD (TWO)

MUSAB rallying the crowd, now using a loudhailer.

MUSAB: Give us the Council of Truth! Give us the People's Choice! Give us the Council of Truth! Give us the People's Choice! Down with Crooked Mahood! Down with Crooked Mahood! Seyyed Hassan for Governor! Seyyed Hassan for Governor!

INTO:

CONFIDENCE

AHMED passes MUSAB on his way into the compound, his face covered. As he reaches RORY he uncovers his face.

RORY: When you came in this morning, did you cover your face?

AHMED: Ah it's nothing.

RORY: Are you being threatened?

AHMED: They put letters through the door. It's happening to all of us.

RORY: When did this start?

AHMED: It's a risk of the job, Rory. These men in the square, they'll get bored. I'm sure of it.

INTO:

THE TABLET

KHALED at the museum, examining something through a magnifying glass.

RORY: I want a clay tablet. I want to put one on display in the Council chamber.

KHALED: Every time my daughter leaves the house, I'm afraid for her and you want me to lend you a clay tablet?

RORY: I want the new Council – the new Governor in particular – to have a sense of the dignity of what they're doing. Show him respect.

KHALED: Seventy-eight goats!

RORY: I'm sorry?

KHALED: That's what it says! The tablet you held up in your precious meeting. That's what we humans are, Rory. We invent writing in order to say 'This is mine'! 'Hands off'!

RORY: Then it's a kind of contract. Better that than you fight over the goats.

INTO:

MUSAB

Just inside the gate of the compound.

RORY and MUSAB.

RORY: Musab – please – I understand you're angry –

MUSAB: You have no understanding of my life.

RORY: The demonstrations are making it difficult to achieve anything. Your brother is now on the Council –

MUSAB: My brother says it is a joke. We copy you, we end up looking like fools.

RORY: It's making progress.

MUSAB: We've been forbidden to speak to you.

RORY: Forbidden? You're free to choose now – look, if you can talk to the crowd, I know they respect you.

RORY begins to get his wallet out –

MUSAB: You want to pay for the truth? The truth is: Leave this country. It's nothing personal Mr Stewart. For your own safety, leave.

INTO:

THEN PRETEND

On the roof of the compound. The noise of the protesters.

RORY and RANA.

RANA: I've written a resignation letter. I think it was a mistake. Me on the Council.

RORY: You're not resigning.

RANA: We haven't agreed anything. Every meeting is just Karim and Seyyed Hassan trading insults.

RORY: It's democracy. Everyone is equally unhappy. It's the defining feature of the system.

RANA: Look at these protesters! Every time I walk in the building they scream at me.

RORY: Hold on a few more days.

RANA: How's that going to help?

RORY: Because then we'll have the turbine.

RANA: That's next month, isn't it?

RORY: Next Wednesday.

RANA: But you told the Council –

RORY: I can't give the real date to the Council. Too much of a security risk. It's a big operation, bringing it in from Kuwait.

RANA: But you're telling me.

RORY: When the turbine comes, people will see what the Council is doing. You can't resign, Rana.

RANA: But I can't speak! In the Council meetings. Four weeks and I haven't said a word. I'm not like you. You have that thing inside you.

RORY: No! You ran your business in Baghdad. You dealt with – I'm going to quote you here – 'roomfuls of bastards'.

RANA: I'm not the person I wanted to be!

RORY: Then pretend. Pretend.

INTO:

FLEXIBILITY

SEYYED HASSAN's office.

SEYYED HASSAN.

RORY: Seyyed. The protests outside the Council building have gone on long enough.

HASSAN: You said you were my best ally.

RORY: The language you're using. It makes it impossible to speak.

HASSAN: You said you would bring us into government.

RORY: And I gave you seats on the Council.

HASSAN: Four!

RORY: You know why that is.

HASSAN: I regret the incident with your friend the seamstress.

RORY: She's not my friend. That was one amongst a number of incidents.

HASSAN: The Council meetings are a disgrace.

RORY: We're taking our first steps.

HASSAN: Like a child?

RORY: Like anything new.

HASSAN: The Council will never succeed with the fool Karim Mahood as its leader.

RORY: And who should replace him, Seyyed? You?

HASSAN: If that is God's will.

RORY: And when another group stages a demonstration, demanding that their leader be made Governor? And the next? And the next? Is that what you want? Whoever assembles the most threatening crowd rules the province?

HASSAN: Says the leader of an occupying army.

RORY: I understand that you feel under-represented on the Council. I'm going to propose that we create a council of religious leaders to advise the main Council –

HASSAN: We've conducted a poll.

RORY: A poll?

SEYYED HASSAN hands an envelope to RORY.

HASSAN: This tells you who the people of Maysan want as Governor.

RORY: You took this poll? Your followers went from house to house asking people who they supported? Were they armed?

HASSAN: This is the truth, clear as a blaze of light. The only question is: do you want to see it?

RORY hands the envelope back to SEYYED HASSAN.

RORY: I'm not going to be held to ransom. A poll is not a vote. Polls are unreliable.

HASSAN: Pontius Pilate asks the Prophet Jesus: What is truth?

RORY: Let's leave Pilate out of this.

HASSAN: But Pilate does not wait for the answer. Why is that, do you think?

RORY: I think he's bewildered. He recognises that Jesus is a holy man. But he's afraid that they're speaking different languages.

HASSAN: He doesn't wait because he doesn't want to know the answer. He wants to believe there is no truth. He thinks it gives him the flexibility he needs to be the Governor of a foreign land.

RORY: Without flexibility, there is no politics.

INTO:

THE PUPPET

RORY's office.

Enter KARIM.

KARIM: You need to clear the square.

RORY: Seyyed Hassan has agreed to speak to his followers.

KARIM: They haven't moved!

RORY: Seyyed Hassan has said he'll ask the protesters to go home.

KARIM: You need to let me station my men outside the Council building.

RORY: We agreed, Karim, that you would leave security to the British Army.

KARIM: And now the Sadrists call me your puppet –

RORY: You're certainly not that –

KARIM: You promised to find the man who killed Abu Rashid. Now I hear you have released the only suspect –

RORY: He had an alibi –

KARIM: The British Military Police have treated him like a kitten.

RORY: We're not going back to the ways of Saddam.

KARIM: I'm the fox. I'm the fox pissing in the sea.

RORY: Karim, wait. The turbine is coming. When it comes –

KARIM: The turbine isn't coming until next month.

RORY: Well. Yes, that's right.

KARIM: Every day we leave these men in the square –

RORY: When the turbine comes, you will make a speech in front of it. Every night, when the streetlights come on, people will see with their own eyes what you have achieved. They will turn to each other and they will say, Karim Mahood did that. The Governor did that.

KARIM: Do you think?

RORY: Wait. Listen.

Pause.

KARIM: My God.

RORY: The chanting's stopped.

INTO:

TRUST

Late night, a few days later.

In the operations room inside the CPA compound, the COLONEL is running the deployment of British troops to deliver the gas turbine up from Kuwait, through Basrah, to the refinery near al-Amarah.

The COLONEL is looking at a laptop, wearing headphones. JT is at a computer, with comms. An air of quiet efficiency.

RORY is watching.

JT: *(Quietly, into headphones.)* Three Zero Charlie. This is Zero. Requesting Sitrep. Over.

Beat.

JT: *(Quietly, into headphones.)* Three Zero Charlie. Roger that. Over. Out. Turbine's on track sir. Be at the refinery at twenty-two-hundred.

COLONEL: That's a good feeling.

JT: She's a beauty, sir.

RORY'S mobile phone rings –

RORY: Excuse me.

RORY answers it –

RORY: Yes I... What?... I'll talk to him now... I'll do that. Absolutely – ... Of course. Of course... Thank you.

Ends call.

RORY: Has Karim tried to contact you?

COLONEL: I haven't spoken to him in days. That was him now?

RORY: He sounded strange. He says there's a gang of men, Sadrists, out on Basrah Street.

COLONEL: We sent a patrol through the centre of town an hour ago.

RORY: He says they're heading north.

COLONEL: Karim saw this?

RORY: He says his brother-in-law saw them going past his house. About twenty men, dressed in black. Led by a man on a horse.

COLONEL: A man on a horse?

RORY: A large, black horse.

COLONEL: What is happening to Karim? Last week he sends us to a Sadrist weapons dump, which turns out to be a fucking garden shed. He's obsessed that the Sadrists are talking to his followers. A man on a horse?

RORY: He said they're heading towards the Council building.

COLONEL: Where he wants us to let him put his men on guard duty?

RORY: We should send out a patrol.

COLONEL: I don't exactly have spare capacity right now.

RORY: We should check.

COLONEL: Rory, we're 45 minutes from delivery.

RORY: I know but –

COLONEL: Seyyed Hassan cleared the square, at your request, right? And his guys on the Council are happy?

RORY: Karim's not lied to me before.

COLONEL: He's lied to both of us the whole time! I mean I like the man, he's one of the bravest men I've met, but. He uses words like toys.

RORY: He sounded different.

COLONEL: A black horse?

RORY: What if he's telling the truth?

COLONEL: OK. Suppose he is. You want me to deploy a patrol at night on Karim's say-so to face an unknown armed force. Anything kicks off we'd struggle to provide backup right now.

RORY: I appreciate that –

COLONEL: Suppose it's a trap? Get us to divert our troops away from the turbine?

RORY: It's the Council building.

COLONEL: It's an empty building! You want me to risk the lives of my men to defend some office furniture?

Beat.

COLONEL: Look Rory. You tell me what you want. You're the senior man here. If this is a formal request to deploy then we can scrape a patrol together. That's the fucking job. But when I do that, I have to know why. I have to know what I'll say to the parents.

RORY: *(Out.)* Karim sounded… afraid. I've never heard that in his voice before.

COLONEL: You believe Karim?

Pause.

RORY: Don't deploy.

COLONEL: OK. Let's get this fucking super-generator delivered and then we can all go to bed.

RORY: I'll call Karim, tell him everything's fine.

COLONEL: Good man. A large black horse! That's one for your next book.

INTO:

ELECTRICITY

The morning.

The room where the Council has been meeting.

Chaos: Tables upended, chairs broken, windows smashed, computer keyboards orphaned, papers strewn.

RORY, RANA and KARIM are surveying the wreckage, righting pieces of furniture.

RORY picks up a knock-off 'NIKEY' baseball cap. Looks at it for a moment, throws it away.

KARIM: This was a loyal desk. This chair served al-Amarah.

RORY: We'll replace everything.

RANA: *(Reading out a flyer picked up from the floor.)* 'We will make our bodies into explosives to shake the old British kingdom.'

KARIM: I told you to shut down their newspaper –

RORY: We can hold today's Council meeting on our compound –

KARIM: Where were your men?

RORY: We sent out a patrol.

KARIM: Your men saw nothing?

RORY: We sent out a patrol earlier in the evening.

KARIM: But after I called you?

RANA: He called you?

RORY: Last night yes –

KARIM: I told you these men were coming.

RANA: You knew this was happening?

KARIM: I do not need you to speak for me.

RORY: We didn't know –

KARIM: I said send out your men –

RORY: The Army was busy last night. On an operation.

KARIM: All of them?

RORY: It was a major operation.

KARIM: I could have stationed my own men outside this building.

RORY: We agreed Karim that your men – [needed further training]

KARIM: Then why didn't you stop them?

RORY: This is only furniture.

KARIM: What are you talking about?

RORY: You're a soldier Karim. You understand that we didn't want to risk soldiers' lives to defend an empty building.

KARIM: What? If this mob had been at the gates of *your* office would your soldiers have stood aside? Whether it was empty or not?

Beat.

RORY: It's not as. It's not as simple as / that.

KARIM: What operation? No one spoke to me –

RORY: The gas turbine. We took delivery last night. You remember I said you should do a – [speech]

KARIM: No, no. It's coming next month.

RORY: It was delivered last night.

KARIM: But you told us next month.

RANA: Oh shit.

RORY: We couldn't tell the whole Council – for security reasons –

KARIM: I don't care about the Council! You didn't tell me. The Governor. Karim Mahood.

Beat.

KARIM: I'm declaring a state of emergency. I'm calling Baghdad –

RORY: Karim –

KARIM: I'm taking direct control of the police force. We will set up a police unit with special powers to combat terrorists –

RORY: Baghdad won't allow you –

KARIM: The Ministry of Information will license all newspapers, television –

RORY: You can't do this.

KARIM: We will arrest Doctor Latif for the murder of Abu Rashid.

RORY: Karim! You have to act within the law.

KARIM: There is no law!

With startling speed, KARIM takes his pistol out of its holster and begins to point it at the three different entrances to the room, sometimes sweeping it across RORY and RANA, neither of whom flinch.

KARIM: You don't understand!

RORY: This is not the way, Karim.

KARIM: You don't see what's happening.

RANA: Please, Karim.

KARIM: You don't see what you've done to me.

RORY: You need to put your gun away.

RANA: Put your gun away, Karim.

KARIM: You didn't send your men. Why didn't you send your men?

RORY: Nothing has happened here. Not yet. Let's go over the road to our compound where we can talk this through. Before you do something you will regret.

SEYYED HASSAN enters with RIFAT.

KARIM jerks his gun back and forth between HASSAN and RIFAT. HASSAN and RIFAT steadily push him back.

KARIM: I've taken emergency powers. The police, newspapers –

HASSAN: Put the gun down, Karim.

KARIM: We will launch a raid. A huge raid.

HASSAN: Come on, Karim.

RORY: Seyyed, this is completely –

RIFAT: Karim Mahood, put your gun away.

RORY: Karim, the police will investigate this act of vandalism and bring those responsible to justice.

HASSAN: *(Ignoring this.)* Look at this invader, Karim. This child.

RORY: Seyyed Hassan, what your men did here last night –

HASSAN: *(Ignoring this.)* You were a fighter against Saddam, while this man was drinking his milk in Scotland.

KARIM: Stop talking to me!

HASSAN: Abu Rashid died for this province –

KARIM: Don't talk about Abu Rashid!

HASSAN: And this man sent him to his death –

RORY: Now democracy is coming.

HASSAN: What are you Karim?

KARIM: I fought against Saddam! I was tortured!

RORY: This is the man who's destroyed your Council building!

HASSAN: And what will they allow you to be?

From here KARIM is pointing his gun at SEYYED HASSAN who walks forward until it is touching his chest.

KARIM: I am a hero of Iraq!

HASSAN: We are not enemies, Karim.

KARIM: I am a good man!

HASSAN: Our enemy is the Iranians, who killed Abu Rashid.

RORY: Don't listen to him –

HASSAN: Our enemy is the lying British Rory Stewart, who treats you with contempt.

KARIM: Stop! Stop!

HASSAN: Together we can fight our enemies.

KARIM: Where is Abu Rashid?

HASSAN: Put the gun down, Karim.

KARIM: Where is my friend Abu Rashid?

HASSAN: Put the gun down.

KARIM: Where is my friend?

HASSAN: Put the gun down.

KARIM slowly lowers his gun. Puts it in its holster.

RORY: Karim, Son of Mahood, Son of Hattab, Sheikh of the great…

HASSAN: *(Signalling to RIFAT to make a call, start a process.)* This is a forty-eight-hour warning. The Crusader Occupiers have forty-eight hours to leave al-Amarah.

RIFAT begins phone call, which carries on under the subsequent dialogue.

RANA: Seyyed –

HASSAN: *(Ignoring this.)* Any Occupier found in the province after that time is a target.

RANA: Seyyed –

HASSAN: What is it? Are you ill?

RANA: For the sake of God, Seyyed, go no further.

HASSAN: Why are you speaking?

RORY: Seyyed –

HASSAN: *(Ignoring this.)* Anyone found co-operating with the Occupiers after that time is a target.

RORY: Don't do this!

HASSAN: *(Ignoring this.)* This building is a symbol of the illegal Occupation. In its destruction we find our beginning.

RORY: You gave me your word –

HASSAN: *(Ignoring this.)* It's time to leave, Karim.

KARIM and RIFAT head to the exit.

RORY: Seyyed Hassan. If you care for. I mean I know that you care for the people of this. The turbine was your idea –

SEYYED HASSAN turns to leave.

RORY: Don't you dare turn your back on me! I am the senior man here and you will listen to me! You gave me your word as a Muslim.

RANA: *(Trying to stop him.)* Rory, don't!

RORY: You are a disgrace to Islam. You dishonour your founder. If you do this Seyyed. Hundreds of your men will die. Thousands. We understand each other. We are alike! There's an election coming! You can stand! Simply stand.

For a moment it looks as if SEYYED HASSAN will respond.

KARIM: What do you think we are made of, that you can shape us with your hands?

Exit KARIM.

HASSAN: *(Out, indicating RORY.)* Do not believe a word this man says.

Then he walks out, followed by RIFAT.

RORY: Stop making decisions and you're dead.

RANA: I need to call my dad. He may want to stay at his cousin's. If this is…happening.

RORY: Stop making –

Enter AHMED at speed, chipper.

AHMED: There's some of the Council members here, wondering what we're – Did something happen? You look like shit.

RANA has got her mobile phone out and begins to dial.

RORY: We need to hold the meeting in the compound. In one hour. Ahmed, you get everyone together –

RANA: Rory, you can stop. It's OK.

RORY: We need a list of no-shows. Call Rifat, remind him he's a member of the Council –

RANA: Rory!

RORY: Call Seyyed Hassan's sheikh, ask him to put pressure –

RANA: Rory! Stop! Stop! Stop.

RANA presses call on her phone.

We hear a mobile phone ring tone answering RANA's call. It's coming from behind a door to one side of the room. A large cleaner's cupboard.

Horrified, everyone is now looking at the door.

RANA: Daddy?

RORY: What?

RORY does not move.

RANA walks over to the door. She stops the call on her phone and the ringing stops.

RANA: Daddy?

She pulls open the door and KHALED tumbles out onto the floor. His face is covered in blood. His eyes particularly.

As KHALED's arm flops out onto the floor, a clay tablet falls out of his hand.

RANA: Daddy?

INTO:

CONTACTS

COLONEL: *(Out.)* In the spring and summer of 2004, the British Army Battle Group stationed in Maysan Province has more contacts with the enemy than any British Army Battle Group since the Korean War.

MUSAB: *(Out.)* I take part in an attempt to storm the wall of the British compound in the centre of the city. In the morning, my brother Rifat collects my body and delivers it to our parents.

COLONEL: *(Out.)* Hundreds of insurgents are killed. The Council splits into warring factions. Jerry Bremer publicly denounces Karim, to no effect.

JT: *(Out.)* We install the turbine. But the grid becomes a favourite target of the insurgents. New gangs of looters emerge. So. *(Shrugs.)*

COLONEL: *(Out.)* They send wave after wave against us. But we hold firm. They calm down. Karim and Seyyed Hassan go their separate ways. As the elections approach, they begin to campaign.

The COLONEL helps RORY to his feet or in some other way offers him a fatherly comfort.

RORY's hand is bloody from helping KHALED.

COLONEL: You OK?

INTO:

DEPARTURES

RORY: *(Out.)* It is 30th of January 2005, the first democratic elections in Iraq.

RORY wipes the blood from his own hands.

RORY begins to clear his desk, collecting together his 'souvenirs' of his time in Iraq: a piece of copper cable, a piece of appliqué, the brochure for the gas turbine, a copy of Thesiger's The Marsh Arabs…

RIFAT, KARIM, SEYYED HASSAN, AHMED, RANA, KHALED all stand before us. RANA supports KHALED, who is wearing black sunglasses.

They dip their index fingers into small white plastic pots of ink.

And then hold out their hands to us, pointing to the sky.

The purple ink stains the fingertip, runs down into the creases of the palm.

The COLONEL hands RORY a job description.

RORY: Stabilisation adviser?

COLONEL: New name. But it's the same job. Development. Politics.

RORY: I'd be based in Helmand?

COLONEL: You like Afghanistan! And you've already been shot at by the Taliban so you've got that out of the way. You think about it: Saddam is sitting in a jail cell and over in that sports hall, they're counting votes. The first Arab democracy, more or less. This has not been a walk in the park, I know that. But if we start to say, this can't be done, what happens next time? If Jordan blows up, the Congo, Syria? What do we do then? Watch as they blow each other into bone meal?

Beat.

COLONEL: Remember: you are a cocky wee shite. That is your God-given state. You're a young man. You need to forgive yourself. Be proud.

Exit the COLONEL.

RORY is left looking at the piece of paper.

SPEAKER: *(Out, the actor speaking.)* At its peak, the coalition in Iraq was spending 150 billion dollars a year, six times the size of the entire Iraqi economy. Nowhere in the last forty years has there been such a concentration of foreign money, manpower, and determination as in Iraq.

AHMED has just entered, perhaps removing his disguise again.

AHMED He's won. Seyyed Hassan has won.

RORY: They're still counting –

AHMED: You can see it already. I just came from the sports hall. The piles of votes! It's – what's the word – an earthquake?

RORY: A landslide.

AHMED: His supporters are all grinning like this.

AHMED does the grin.

RORY: But – what about Karim?

AHMED: Nothing.

RORY: Nothing?

AHMED: I suppose you'd say, he was theatre.

RORY: Seyyed Hassan won?

AHMED: *(Out, the actor speaking.)* My character is based on Haider al-Maliki, a young English Literature graduate who was one of Rory's Iraqi translators. A year from now, in early 2006, he will be dragged from his car, almost certainly by members of an Islamist militia, and shot dead. His favourite author was Mister George Bernard Shaw.

RORY: I'm sorry, Ahmed.

AHMED: Don't be sorry, Rory! It's not an easy road but – look at this!

AHMED holds up his finger, dyed with ink.

AHMED: You gave us that!

Exit AHMED.

SPEAKER: *(Out, the actor speaking.)* In the years since 2005, the electorate of Maysan province, like all the provinces of southern Iraq, has continued to elect Islamist politicians, who have an anti-Western agenda, implement conservative social codes and keep armed militas.

SPEAKER: *(Out, the actor speaking.)* The current governor is Ali Dawai Lazem, a Sadrist.

RANA and KHALED at home.

A light burning.

The light flickers.

RORY holds out a document – funding paperwork.

RORY: This funds your class for the next year.

RANA: Your last day?

RORY: I just need you to sign and.

RANA: Back to Scotland. See your family.

RORY: I want to know you'll be able to carry on.

RANA: And then? Your next mountain pass?

RORY: Take the money. It'll allow you to carry on for –

RANA: And if they come to shut my class?

RORY: I don't. I don't know.

RANA: You've destroyed our world.

RORY: Sign the papers and we can –

RANA: This is our house. I want you to leave. I want you to leave our house.

KHALED: Rana, darling. He's our guest. He's in this house as our guest.

Outside, gunfire in the distance.

The lights flicker.

KHALED: He is our guest.

JT enters.

JT picks up RORY's box of souvenirs and takes it away.

RORY leaves Maysan.

INTO:

NOW

RORY now, in Scotland, among his trees.

RORY: *(Out.)* It is April 2017. I'm forty-four years old. Middle-aged. What do we know? What can we do? What do we have the right to do? We arrive, thinking we are superheroes. We leave…

The End.

ACKNOWLEDGEMENTS

A long journey gathers many debts.

Over the years of working on *Occupational Hazards*, I have benefited from reading the work of George Packer, Wendell Steavenson, Wilfred Thesiger, Rajiv Chandrasekaran, Dan Mills, Gavin Maxwell, Norman Lewis, Kanan Makiya, Patrick Cockburn and Thomas Ricks, among many other writers and journalists.

Thank you to Hilary Synnott, Jeremy Condor, Luke Baker and others who spoke to me in the UK; to the people I met in the offices of Islamic Dawa in London and Moqtada al-Sadr and Ayatollah Ali al-Sistani in Damascus; and to all the Iraqi refugees I interviewed in Damascus in 2009, who were warm and welcoming no matter their views or circumstances, and in particular my translator-fixers, Firas Majeed, Rana al-Aiouby and Roula Nasrallah.

Thank you to Anna Girvan, Tom Lyons and especially Emily Burns for great dramaturgy; to Tom Morris, Emma Stenning and Will Adamsdale for launching the project; to the actors who read the script at the NT Studio and at the Hampstead; to all the friends who commented on the script in draft, in particular Samantha Ellis, Abigail Burdess, Jesse Fox, Paul King, John Nathan, Laura Barber, Lotte Wakeham and Marie Phillips; and to Robbie Hudson, who read and commented on the script many, many times.

Thank you to Ed Hall, Greg Ripley-Duggan, Will Mortimer and everyone at Hampstead Theatre for giving *Occupational Hazards* a good home. Thank you to our terrific cast and creative team, who have helped so much with the final shaping of the script. Thank you particularly to Henry Lloyd-Hughes for taking it all magnificently in his stride. Thank you to Rosie Cobbe for being a brilliant agent.

Thank you most of all to two dear friends: Simon Godwin, who has brought his passion and vision to the script and the production; and Rory himself, who let me adapt his memoir and then gave me the best gift an adaptor could ask for: a free hand.

***

As noted at the beginning, this play uses dramatic licence to turn Rory Stewart's memoir into a story for the stage. Those seeking to disentangle truth and art should look in the first instance to Rory's book; beyond that, to journalism and other accounts.

But I want to acknowledge here a few particular choices in adaptation: that I have omitted Molly Phee – who became Rory's boss part way through our story – and many others who worked alongside Rory; that I have greatly simplified Iraqi Shia politics, leaving out the parties that were, to varying degrees, more friendly towards the Coalition than the Sadrists; that I have ignored the six-monthly rotation of British Army Battle Groups in Iraq; and that I have raised the fluency of Rory's Arabic and thus reduced the role of his translators.

I stand by these choices. I assume that these kinds of omission are an unavoidable part of the adaptor's job. But, given the bravery and suffering of so many of those I have chosen to leave out, I want to mark their absence here.

WWW.OBERONBOOKS.COM

Follow us on www.twitter.com/@oberonbooks
& www.facebook.com/OberonBooksLondon